Polymer Clay

ROCKPORT

First published in the United States of America by
Rockport Publishers, Inc.
33 Commercial Street
Gloucester, Massachusetts 01930-5089
Telephone: (978) 282-9590
Fax: (978) 283-2742
www.rockpub.com

Library of Congress Cataloging-in-Publication Data

Sargeant, Georgia.

Polymer clay : exploring new techniques and new materials / Georgia Sargeant, Celie Fago, and Livia McRee.

p.   cm.

ISBN 1-56496-869-3 (pbk.)

1. Polymer clay craft. I. Fago, Celie. II. McRee, Livia, [date] III. Title.

TT297.S25   2002

731.4'2–dc21   2001007611

10 9 8 7 6 5 4 3 2 1

Design and Production: *tabula rasa* graphic design
Cover Image: Bobbie Bush Photography
Photography: Bobbie Bush, except where noted
Illustrator: Lorraine Dey
Copy Editor: Stacey Follin
Proofreader: Pamela Angulo

Printed in China

Polymer Clay

EXPLORING NEW TECHNIQUES AND NEW MATERIALS

GLOUCESTER MASSACHUSETTS

ROCKPORT PUBLISHERS

Georgia Sargeant and Celie Fago
with Livia McRee

Contents

Exploring Polymer Clay
by Georgia Sargeant

Polymer clay is solid color—color you can knead, twist, pull, mold, layer, and cut. You can make it look like ancient amber, glowing glass, engraved ivory, or modern steel. You can use it to make delicate miniatures or large folding screens, wrap it around an armature, or stretch it out to airy thinness. You can layer it with metal leaf, blend in scented spices or delicate sparkles, transfer photocopied images on to it, or tint the surface with paint and colored pencil. It is wonderfully convenient because it will harden in twenty minutes in a home oven, so expensive studio space and fiery kilns are not needed. A corner of a table in a small apartment will do just fine.

In recent years, polymer clay has been transformed from a child's toy to a mature art medium, yet its delightful playfulness has not been lost. It can be bright or dull, large or small, realistic or abstract, down to earth or fantastical. It has been used to make jewelry, dolls, sculptures, accessories, wearable art, lamps, books, boxes, and bowls; it has been turned into mosaics, plaques, wall hangings, furniture, and decorations.

Polymer clay is a modern material that combines well with other media, allowing you to borrow techniques and tools from other arts and industries and use them in your own creations. In turn, modeling and construction techniques devised for polymer clay can be applied to other media, especially precious metal clay, producing metal objects with a fluidity and freshness seldom attained before. In the first section of this book, eleven artists will introduce you to decorative and structural techniques for polymer clay. In the second section, master craftsman Celie Fago will show you how to work in PMC and how to combine it with polymer clay. In the Gallery section, many artists will show you examples of how some of these techniques have been used in creating marvelous and evocative objects to delight the senses and entice the imagination.

The projects in this book are intended to explore the wide-ranging possibilities of this versatile medium. There is something for everyone—from those just starting to discover polymer clay to those who have been creating with it for a while and are ready to experiment with new techniques. Keep in mind that the most beautiful and ingenious polymer clay techniques were developed by fellow enthusiasts—we hope that this book inspires you to develop a few of your own.

Polymer Clay Basic Techniques

Polymer clay is a brilliantly colored modern modeling material that bakes hard in a home oven. Its star feature is its compatibility with other art and craft materials, from acrylic paints to glues to glitter to metal leafing to rubber-stamping supplies. With polymer clay, sturdy and colorful three-dimensional art is within everyone's reach. It's widely available in art and craft stores.

The basic ingredient of polymer clay is polyvinyl chloride (PVC), the same sturdy stuff that water pipes are made of. The other ingredients are inert fillers to give it bulk (and sometimes texture), dyes and pigments to give it color, and a plasticizer—an oily chemical that allows the microscopic chains of PVC molecules to slide over each other at room temperature but lock onto each other when the clay is heated.

This clay, also known to its fans as "polyclay" and "PC," comes in many of the colors you find on the artist's paint rack—not only in standard colors like red, white, and brown, but also in flesh tones (developed for doll making) and in translucent clays that are milky when raw but almost clear when baked properly (and in a thin enough layer, they're absolutely transparent). With many brands, you can mix the package colors and get attractive intermediate shades.

Manufacturers also make some wonderful specialty clays. There are pearlescent and metallic colors incorporating tiny mica flakes that give a shimmery luster. There are fluorescent colors using brilliant pigments; a dab added to a dull color will perk it up. There are glow-in-the-dark colors that shine at night. There are glitter clays—tinted translucent clays with heat-resistant microfine glitter mixed in. There are clays that contain short colored fibers that make them look like stone. You can even make your own stone clays by mixing embossing powder from the rubber-stamp counter into translucent clay. Or you can mix in other grains or powders, from coffee grounds to aromatic herbs to iridescent pigments to children's tinted play sand.

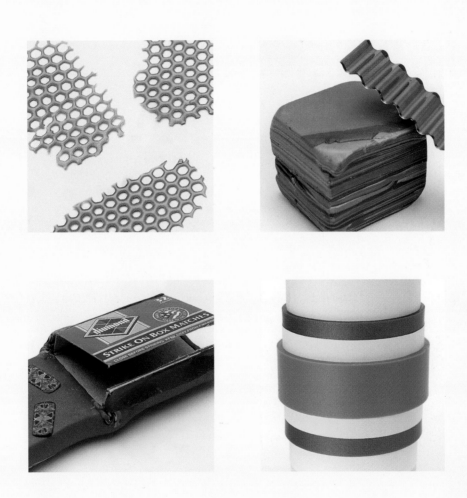

Which Clay Should You Use?

Polymer clay is colorful, adaptable, and compatible with many other art and craft materials. It's heat-sensitive, which means it's stiff when cold and more malleable when warm. As you knead and condition it, especially by hand, it gets warmer and softer and stickier, but it does firm up again when it cools.

The different brands on the market are similar enough to be blended successfully, but they do have different characteristics. Become familiar with the various properties of each, and it will be easy to choose the right clay for the job. Manufacturers do change clay formulas from time to time, and they're always releasing new products, so test clays yourself to discover your favorite.

- **Sculpey** is an inexpensive, soft, brittle white clay that is popular with railroad and dollhouse modelers for making buildings and landscape figures that will not receive wear and tear. It takes paint well.

- **Sculpey III** bakes to an attractive matte finish, and its translucent clay becomes the clearest of all. It's often given to children because it's soft out of the package. However, it can accidentally "toast," or turn brown, if the oven temperature is too high, and it's relatively chalky and brittle even when properly baked, so it breaks easily if dropped.

- **Premo Sculpey** is a fine all-purpose clay that is strong and slightly flexible when properly baked. Many of the colors are the same as artist's paint colors, making paint-mixing savvy useful. It's a good caning clay. Some sculptors and doll makers find it too soft and sticky.

- **Sculpey Super Flex** is a very soft and sticky clay when uncured, yet it remains highly flexible even after it's baked. If you want to make a mold from an existing object, you must ensure that the object and the clay won't stay stuck together by first coating the clay with a release agent such as cornstarch, baby powder, talcum powder, water, or glycerin.

- **Super Sculpey** is a very strong, hard clay designed for doll making. It's sold only in large packages.

- **Liquid Sculpey,** which is flexible and waterproof once cured, is also available. It comes in translucent and opaque formulas, and it's a wonderful transfer medium. It can be used in many ways, such as bonding cured clay to raw clay and coating fragile

materials like lace and leaves. It also makes a good glaze if baked soon after application.

- **Fimo** was the first polymer clay on the market, and it may still be the most widely distributed. It's made by Eberhardt Faber, a German art supplies manufacturer. It's an excellent all-purpose clay.

- **Fimo Classic** is the firmest clay, valued by cane makers for its ability to hold fine patterns and by sculptors for its ability to take sharp details and hold its shape.

- **FimoSoft** is firm in the package but pressure-sensitive, so it softens readily under a roller. The transparent colors are brilliant, like stained glass. The glitter colors are made from tinted transparent clay blended with fine, heat-tolerant glitter.

- **Cernit** is formulated for doll making. It's soft to handle, but it's the hardest of the polymer clays when cured. Most colors are slightly translucent, like porcelain.

- **Creall-Therm** is excellent for making miniatures, because it can safely be rolled out into tiny threads without breaking, and it isn't overly sticky.

Basic Polymer Clay Equipment and Supplies

Along with traditional art tools, many household items can be been adapted for use with polymer clay. Experiment, and you'll soon discover which ones you like best. Below are the essential items you'll need to begin.

Safety Tip: Polymer clay is certified nontoxic, so it's safe for adults and supervised children to use. However, once you use a kitchen tool with polymer clay, don't use it for preparing food again, and don't place damp foods on polymer clay surfaces.

Basic Kit

- **(A) Work surface.** A large, smooth, and solvent-proof work area is your base. It can be made of Plexiglas, tempered glass, marble, tile, Formica, or similar kitchen counter material; even a cloudy, flexible polypropylene plastic cutting board or heavy paper or cardboard will serve. Don't use a varnished tabletop; raw clay will damage varnish and acrylic plastics like those used for inexpensive picture frames. Bare wood isn't ideal,

either, because clay will stick in the pores. If you use paper for your work area, you'll need a separate cutting surface made from Lucite, glass, or a self-healing craft cutting board.

- **(B) Rolling tools.** A Plexiglas pipe or rod, brayer, heavyweight straight-sided drinking glass or jar, thick wooden dowel, or marble rolling pin will all work. To make large, even, thin sheets, a pasta machine (shown on page 12) is extremely helpful.

- **(C) Cutting tools.** Sharp scissors with smooth blades, craft knives with pointed and rounded blades, and long, thin tissue blades specially made for polymer clay are all useful.

Safety Tip: Tissue blades are extremely sharp, and both the dull and cutting edge look similar. Paint the dull side with nail polish, or bake a strip of polymer clay on a corner for a handle. Remove, then glue the handle into place once baked to secure it.

- **(D) Needle and Sculpting tools.** These are available from ceramics suppliers and can also be found in the sculpting sections of art supply stores. You can also make your own needle tool by placing a large darning needle in a polymer clay ball, baking it, then pulling out the needle, washing off any oil, and gluing it back in place with cyanoacrylate glue. Knitting needles and wooden skewers are also useful.

- **Oven.** When you're first getting to know polymer clay, a home oven may be used, then wiped out and washed down carefully afterward. Once hooked, most cautious clay lovers find themselves a small portable toaster oven or convection oven and use it only for art. (Not shown).

- **Oven thermometer.** In order to properly cure polymer clay, check and calibrate your oven's temperature. (Not shown).

- **Rubbing alcohol.** Tools and surfaces should be cleaned using alcohol. (Not shown).

- **Finishing materials.** Wet/dry sandpaper is used to create the gorgeous, polished finish on many of the projects in this book. You'll need grades ranging from 320 to 600, which you can buy from home improvement stores. For an even shiner finish, extra-fine grades from 800 to 2,000 are available from auto-supply stores. (Not shown).

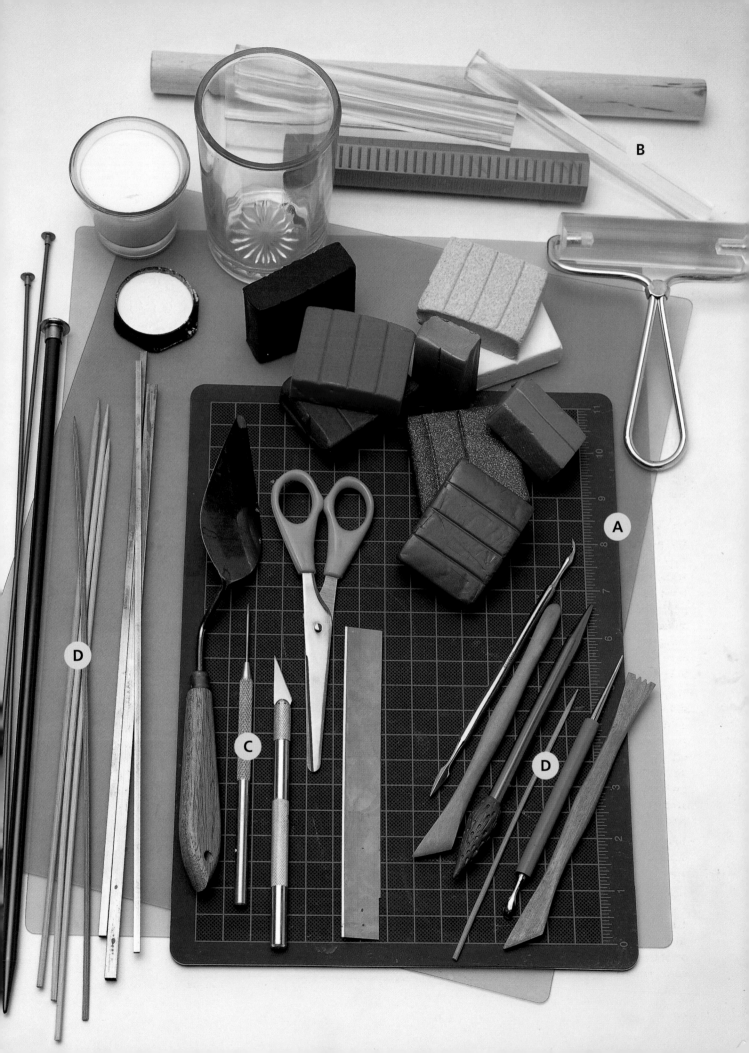

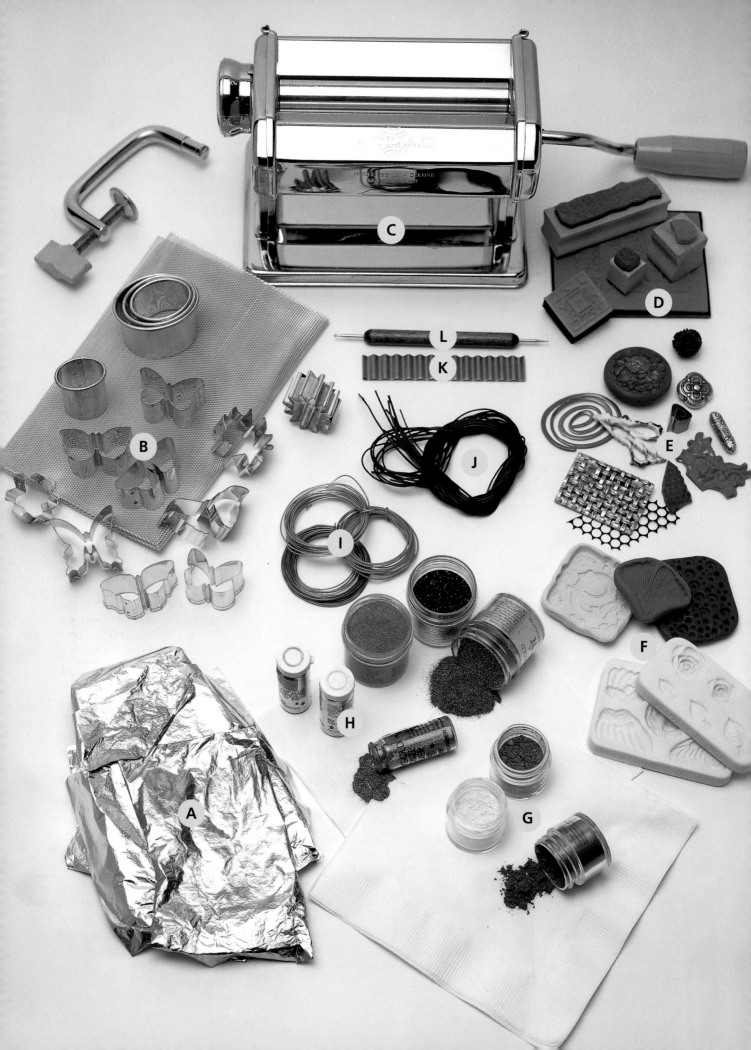

• **Latex or plastic gloves.** Polymer clay is certified nontoxic, but like all art materials, it should be used with care. Some people find it irritates the skin of their hands, so protect yours with latex or plastic gloves, or an artists' or mechanics' cream. (Not shown).

Intermediate Kit

Listed below are some of the things that can also be used with polymer clay. Many of the items pictured here are called for in the projects that follow. Once you've assembled a basic kit, start experimenting with other materials to assemble a more sophisticated, personalized kit.

- **(A) Metallic leaf**
- **(B) Cookie and hors d'ouevres cutters**
- **(C) Pasta machine (durable Italian model)**
- **(D) Deep-cut rubber stamps, line images**
- **(E) Texturing tools, such as beads, charms, found objects**
- **(F) Molds, handmade and commercial**
- **(G) Powders and pigments, such as metallic, mica, and embossing powders**
- **(H) Inclusions, such as ultra-fine glitters and tiny beads**
- **(I) Plastic-coated craft wire**
- **(J) Rubber and leather cording**
- **(K) Wavy blade**
- **(L) Ball-end stylus**

Working with Polymer Clay
Conditioning

Polymer clay can be used right out of the package, but artists have found that conditioning it by kneading makes it stronger and more pliable. During conditioning, the plasticizer is distributed more evenly, bubbles are driven out, and the clay warms up and softens. When it cools it will firm up again, but the other improvements will remain.

To condition clay by hand, it's best to start with your clay at body temperature. To get it there, you can put the packages in your clothing for a while or place them in a gentle warming device such as a baby-bottle warmer, or you can seal them in a zip-top plastic bag and submerge the bag in lukewarm water.

Remove the wrapper, and lay about an ounce of clay—half a block—on your work surface. Roll over it heavily using a strong roller: a Plexiglas rod or pipe, a brayer, a thick wooden dowel, or a rolling pin. Squash it flat, fold it, and roll again.

When it's a bit softer, form it into a log and roll it out into a snake, fold it over and twist it, and ball it up. Repeat until the clay has the texture and elasticity you want—15 to 20 times.

To condition clay with the pasta machine, lay half a block of clay on your work surface and flatten it as above, to make it thin enough to feed into the pasta machine's rollers. Crank it through on the machine's widest setting. Fold the resulting sheet in half and feed it through again, fold first. Repeat about 20 times.

It takes the same amount and kind of work to condition clay as to mix colors uniformly. If you want to mix colors, start when you start conditioning.

Leaching

Clay that is fresh from the factory may be too soft and sticky to work with. To harden it a bit, roll it into sheets (use the middle thickness on your pasta machine) and place them on clean office paper, then sandwich that between absorbent newspapers, weight it down with books, and leave for at least 24 hours. Some of the oily plasticizer will leach into the papers. In some cases you may have to do this more than once before the clay is firm enough for you.

Softening

All clay becomes firmer over time, as polymerization slowly advances. Some clays are inherently stiffer than others. Vegetable oil, mineral oil, and two proprietary softeners—Sculpey Diluent and Fimo Mix Quick—can be used to soften clay that is too hard. First, chop up the hard clay, place it in a zip-top plastic bag, add a few drops of softener, and leave it to soak in overnight. Then, the next day, compress the bag to stick the clay scraps together, take them out and place them on a sheet of fresh clay, fold the sheet around the scraps, and condition the whole sandwich.

Storing Opened Packages

Don't leave raw clay on a painted or varnished surface, because the plasticizer will mar the surface. Instead, store the clay in the original package or in a polyethylene bag. A polyethylene shoebox makes a good storage container because the plasticizer in the clay has no effect on polyethylene. (Polyethylene is the plastic used for grocery and sandwich bags, recognizable because it's translucent and quite flexible, especially when it's thin). The box also protects the clay from dust.

Baking

Each manufacturer provides specifications for baking, or curing, their brand of polymer clay properly so it hardens and fuses throughout without burning. These specifications are printed on the packages, and they vary from brand to brand. If the directions are missing, a good rule of thumb is to bake your clay project for 20 minutes per ¼" (6 mm) of thickness at 265° F to 275° F (129° C to 135° C). Some of the translucent clays will brown at this temperature, so first bake a test tile the same thickness as your project.

Most ovens cycle, first heating above the designated temperature, then turning off the heat and cooling down, then heating again. Most oven thermometers are inaccurate. To control the temperature, preheat the oven and use a separate oven thermometer to calibrate it. Adjust the dial on the oven until the oven thermometer reads 265° F (129° C), and don't worry about what the dial says.

If your oven has an overhead heating element, you may want to protect your project from scorching with an aluminum foil tent. You really don't want the clay to go above 300° F (149° C), because it will begin to scorch and emit unpleasant-smelling fumes.

During baking, the clay goes through a soft stage when it can sag or slump under gravity and conform to the surface supporting it. To prevent this, thin strands or sheets should be supported with a curl of paper, and to avoid getting glassy spots where the clay piece has touched a polished glass or metal baking surface, it's a good idea to lay the clay on a piece of plain paper or cardboard for baking.

Beads can be set on pleated paper or cardstock, which will yield while supporting them; or they can be held up on a bamboo skewer, a stiff wire, or 00 aluminum knitting needles. Large rounded objects can be supported during baking in a nest of polyester quilt stuffing, which won't melt or stick to the clay.

Ceramic tiles make excellent, inexpensive, portable baking surfaces, and they're available in both glossy and matte finishes. Many clayers bake on metal or tempered glass pans or sheets of cardboard. Don't bake on Teflon, which can fuse with polymer clay.

After baking, most projects should be allowed to cool slowly to room temperature. But translucent clay benefits from being dropped into ice water while still hot; if you do this, the final project will appear more translucent.

Cleaning Up

Your work surface and pasta machine should be kept clean to avoid having one color clay contaminate the next one. Many clayers wipe down their machines with baby wipes (premoistened cleaning towelettes) or rubbing alcohol poured on a paper towel.

The warmer your hands, the more likely they are to acquire a sticky film of clay as you work. Massaging in a little hand lotion and wiping it off with a paper towel, then washing with cool water and dish detergent that cuts grease well should do the trick.

Basic Techniques

Making Sheets

Many decorative and structural techniques require sheets of a certain size and shape. The easiest way to control this is to pinch and pull your conditioned clay into a rough rectangle about the thickness of a dinner plate, then roll it through a pasta machine, which is designed to roll out even, consistent layers of dough. Pasta machines take so much of the labor out of clay work that they're well worth the investment—and they can often be found at secondhand stores and yard sales.

But even if you don't have a pasta machine, you can still make thin even sheets by using bakers' techniques and treating your clay like pie crust dough. With your hands, roll a lump of conditioned clay into a fat round cylinder; dust it with cornstarch or talc; and flatten it with a thick roller. You can pull on the edges with your hands to help the process.

When the clay gets pretty thin, tape down two long rods, skewers, or chopsticks beside the clay in a parallel orientation. Many hobby shops sell foot-long sections of squared-off brass and aluminum tubing, in different diameters, that would be ideal for this. Then roll your clay out even with the rods. You can use these rods to make another sheet of the same thickness whenever you want.

Millefiori (Canework)

One of polymer clay's most popular techniques comes from its ability to stretch evenly and smoothly. It shares this quality, technically known as "thixotropicity," with hot glass and hard candy. This stretchiness makes it possible to layer several colors together in a pattern, consolidate the layers into a multicolored loaf, then stretch out the loaf without changing the proportions of the colors. These multicolored loaves are called canes (think candy canes).

Long pieces of different-colored polymer clay can be assembled into many-colored "canes" that keep the same pattern throughout the length, even after you compress the sides and stretch the cane out long and narrow. This is called "reducing" the cane—really you're reducing the diameter but increasing the length. The great thing is that with clay, unlike glass or hard candy, you can do it all at room temperature! And once you have made a cane, you can make many thin slices with the same pattern, like slicing a jelly-roll dessert and getting the same spiral pattern in every slice. And in fact, one of the most common canes is called a jelly-roll cane.

Cane patterns can be as simple as stripes, checks, bull's-eyes, and swirls. And because you can stack and pack simple canes together, they can also add up to complex canes of flowers, faces, and even landscapes. See the Chrysanthemum Cane Heart Pendants on page 26 for an easy, beautiful cane project.

Color Mixing, Marbling, and Blends

You can mix two or more colors during the conditioning process simply by flattening each color and stacking the layers to begin with; by the time you have finished conditioning, the colors will be mixed.

One of the simplest decorative techniques is to marble the clay. Start by making small snakes of different colors of conditioned clay. Bundle them, pack them, and twist them together. Roll the bundle on your work surface to lengthen it, then fold and twist again. Stop when you like the marbled effect; if you go too far, the clay will start to look blended rather than marbled.

PASTA MACHINE SETTINGS

Many of the projects in this book specify using a pasta machine for conditioning clay or for rolling out uniform layers. This chart lists the corresponding thickness for each setting of the Atlas brand machine, a common and sturdy brand. Some machines have more than seven settings.

Setting #	Inches	Millimeters
#1	1/8"	3.2 mm
#2	7/64"	2.8 mm
#3	3/32"	2.4 mm
#4	5/64"	2 mm
#5	1/16"	1.6 mm
#6	1/32"	0.8 mm
#7	1/40"	0.6 mm

WHICH GLUE SHOULD YOU USE?

PVA-based white craft glue	Use this basic glue to help raw clay bond to baked clay or stick to paper. PVA stands for polyvinyl acetate, a close chemical cousin to the PVC (polyvinyl chloride) that is the basis of polymer clay. Coat the other surface with the glue and allow it to dry, then affix the raw clay.
Cyanoacrylate glue	Sometimes called super-glue, this glue can be used to bond baked clay to metal, glass, or other pieces of baked clay. Clean metal findings with alcohol to ensure a good bond. Don't bake cyanoacrylate glue— the bond fails at high temperatures.
E6000 silicon glue	This heavy-duty glue is extremely effective, but it contains harsh solvents. Use it outdoors.
Two-part epoxy glue	These glues are good for bonding baked clay to metal, such as jewelry findings.

True blends that shade smoothly from one color to another were first devised by artist Judith Skinner. For a **simple blend,** start by rolling out clay sheets about the same size in two colors. (The clay need not be conditioned in advance, because it will be conditioned by the blending process.) Trim them into rectangles. Slice one sheet diagonally, and stack the two triangles; repeat with the other. Butt the two double triangles together so they make a rectangle, one color on each side; overlap the edge a bit, and press them so they stick together. Feed the double-thick rectangle through the rollers of the pasta machine. This will stretch out the rectangle twice as long but a single thickness. Fold it in half again at the "waist" and roll it through again, fold first. Repeat about 15 times, always folding at the waist and sending it through fold first. By the time you have finished, you'll have a smooth color blend with one color down one vertical edge and the other color down the other vertical edge; the upper and lower edges will show the blend.

For a **complex blend,** start by rolling out a clay sheet at least 6" (15 cm) long in each color you want to use. From each sheet, cut out two long triangles about 2" (5 cm) wide at the base. Assemble them together head-to-foot into a rectangle the width of your pasta machine; overlap the edges of the pieces, and pinch them to tack them together. Send the whole through the pasta machine. Fold the long rectangle at the "waist," and send it through the pasta machine, fold first. Repeat as above. You'll have a blended sheet with one color down one side, another down the other side, with all the other colors between; the top and bottom edges will show the blend. (If you stop early—after about 10 times—you'll have an incomplete blend with a cross-section that looks streaky, like Ikat cloth.)

Metallic Effects

Some of the Premo brand clays contain so much mica that they look like mother-of-pearl or metal. Mica is formed of flat plates, and remarkably, when you run the metallic or pearl clays through the pasta machine, the pressure seems to make the plates line up and face the surface of the sheet. Because the little plates reflect light, the surface looks brighter and brighter the more you send it through the pasta machine. Conversely, the edges of the sheet look darker because you're looking between the little plates.

Artists discovered this effect and figured out many ways to use it. Most rely on making sheets of brightened clay, cutting them into uniform

pieces, stacking them, and then manipulating the stack in various ways to take advantage of the contrast between the brightened surface and the darkened edges.

The ghost image is one of the most magical of the metallic techniques. Pressing a deeply cut line-image rubber stamp or a texture sheet into the top of a brightened sheet will disturb the alignment of the little plates, so the impressed marks look darker. If you use a sharp blade to take paper-thin slices off the very surface of the sheet, then send the sheet back through the pasta machine, you can still see a ghost of the image! The Textured Ikebana Vase project on page 30 takes advantage of this effect.

> **Artist's Tip:** Mike Buesseler makes a stack of mica-rich polymer clay two or three sheets thick and cuts it into strips as wide as they are thick. On each strip, the top and bottom are bright and the sides are dark. When he twists the strips to make beads, the contrast between the dark and light surfaces really sets off the twist.

Mokumé Gané

An ancient Japanese metalworking technique inspired the artists who developed these methods. The original involved soldering and compressing layers of several colored metals into one fused piece, punching into them from both sides to make bumps and hollows, then sanding off the bumps to reveal the layers beneath.

In clay, of course, it's easy to get different layers to stick together, and clay artists have a rainbow of colors, translucents, pearly clays, paints, inclusions, and metal leaf to work with. Different artists have developed special variations on the theme. Layer work shows how different artists can take a basic idea, play with it, and come up with utterly different results.

The core mokumé gané technique is to stack different colored sheets of unbaked clay, rumple them like a bed after a restless night or punch into them, then take thin slices from the top. Because the layers are no longer flat, each cut will slice through several layers, revealing striations the way a road cut reveals underlying layers of earth and stone, or a wood carver reveals the grain of a block of wood. Often these irregular slices are flipped over, laid on another sheet of clay, and rolled down to create a variegated sheet. This can be used as is or made into a

> **Artist's Tip:** Nan Roche's version of mokumé gané , affectionately called Nan gané , starts with three or more thin sheets of opaque clay in strongly contrasting colors and shades, such as gold and black and red. She stacks these sheets, runs them through the pasta machine at its thickest setting, cuts the resulting sheet in half, stacks the pieces, runs them through again, and then repeats the process. This process yields a 12-ply sheet about ⅛" (3 mm) thick (you don t want to go too far or the layers will be too thin to show clearly). Nan likes to press this sheet over a shallow mold such as the matrix board for a custom-made rubber stamp of ancient writing. When she slices off the raised areas, the letter forms appear in a halo of concentric layers. See page 115 for an example.

veneer to cover an object. Depending on which clays are originally selected and whether other materials such as glitter or metal leaf are included, the effects can be very different.

Using Armatures, Inside and Out

Polymer clay is malleable until cured, and it becomes even softer for a short time during baking. Small objects usually aren't heavy enough to go out of shape during baking, but heat and gravity will make sheets and large items sag unless they're supported.

Heavy paper and cardboard can be used externally—for example, a stiff paper cone can be wrapped in a floppy sheet of clay, which will be sturdy once it has been baked. Heat-resistant materials can be used internally, as armatures. Glass and most metals are suitable. Crushed aluminum foil makes a good core for sculptures and beads. Metal screening such as WireForm can be used to reinforce thin sheets.

With successive bakings, clay itself can become a kind of armature. After the foundation layer is baked, it becomes stiff and easy to handle; later layers can be added and baked, permitting the construction of elaborate objects. A tiny dab of Translucent Liquid Sculpey on points that may be stressed later will help ensure a solid bond between baked and raw clay.

Covering Forms

When a sheet of clay is wrapped or draped over a glass, metal, wood, or cardboard form and then baked, the clay takes on that shape. You can use found objects like bottles, bowls, boxes, lighting fixtures, switch plates, or tins as forms, or you can build your own with tape and cardboard.

If you don't want the clay and the form to stick together after baking, use a release agent between them. Pull the clay and form apart while they're still hot from baking; clay expands very little when hot, but that little can be helpful in separating tightly fitted pieces. If you're willing to leave the form in place, simple enclosure will hold them together. If you don't want to leave it in, you can cut the clay (preferably an angled cut), pull out the form, and then use glue or TLS to reunite the cuts. Don't use varnished or painted metal as a form without a lot of release agent; the clay will stick to the varnish. Conversely, painted tins can easily be permanently covered with clay because it sticks to the paint.

Making Molds

Well-conditioned polymer clay makes excellent rigid molds. You need to use a release agent—that is, anything that will cover the object you're molding but won't stick to the clay, such as water, waxed paper or office paper, metal leaf, ArmorAll (a protectant for car interiors), glycerin, cornstarch, talcum powder, and mica powders. When using a wet release, put it on the object. When using a powdery release, put it on the clay. Avoid objects with undercuts or overhangs; the clay will wrap around them, and you won't be able to get it off after baking. If you're using cornstarch, you can wad up your clay and start over if you make a mistake. If you're using ArmorAll, that may not work; it won't mix in. ArmorAll works so well as a release that if you use it to coat a baked clay mold, you can actually bake a raw clay casting in the mold (which would otherwise be impossible because the raw clay would stick to the baked clay).

To make a flat mold of a small object, start with a good big piece of well-conditioned scrap clay left over from an earlier project (use new clay if you don't have scrap clay). It's usually easier to put the object on the table, powder the clay thoroughly, and press it down over the object. If necessary, press the object down into the clay. Your mold should be at least ¼" (6 mm) thick, with a thick lip. If the object is heatproof, like glass or metal, you can leave it in during baking and get a very crisp mold. If the object isn't heatproof, like plastic, or if you aren't sure whether it has undercuts, loosen the clay gently and pull out the object before baking the mold. The longer you bake it, the tougher it will be.

To make a full-round mold of a three-dimensional object such as a bead, start with a thick

flat pad of clay coated with cornstarch or ArmorAll. Push the object halfway in. Press a rounded item such as a pencil eraser down into the surface, separate from the object, in two places. Bake the mold for about 10 minutes, just enough to harden, and let it cool. Make a similar pad of clay, and coat it well with mold release. Press it down over the object and the baked clay, and into the rounded holes you made (these will help your mold halves fit together properly). Bake for 10 minutes; cool and remove the object. Rebake the halves of the mold for at least an hour. Later, when you make a casting in the mold, there may be a seam line (called flashing). Use a sharp craft knife to trim it off before baking the casting.

What objects make good molds? Most things that were originally stamped out or made in molds—such as brass charms, old jewelry, or cut-glass buttons—can be used to produce molds. Pressed into raw clay, rubber stamps function as shallow molds, and the matrix boards in which they're made are also molds; you can have your own stamps made and get back both the rubber and the matrix board. You can make your own polymer clay texture molds using found objects and surfaces ranging from leaves and feathers to stones to industrial surfaces to kitchen tools. Commercial molds for making dolls and polymer clay items are available, and you can try molds made for soap, plaster, candy, cookies, and sugarcraft.

There are also materials on the market for making flexible molds. These can be used on objects with undercuts because you can stretch the mold to get it off the object. Silicon molding materials for jewelers and dentists make excellent, detailed molds, but they can be expensive. The pendant project on page 54 will show you how to make a mold using Super Elasticlay, a polymer clay developed for mold making that remains flexible after baking.

Embellishments and Surface Treatments
Inclusions

To liven up the smooth uniformity of clay as it comes from the package, you can add chopped or powdered materials—grains, coffee grounds, tea leaves, aromatic herbs, sand, fibers, chopped crayons—virtually anything. Just be sure the material is completely dry and nonreactive.

When adding inclusions, the basic idea is to cover and enfold them, catching a minimum of air. Roll out a good-sized, fairly thick sheet of clay. Pour a small amount of the inclusion

material into the middle of the sheet, then fold it over the material and pinch most of the sides closed, leaving a corner or two open. Gently press the folded sheet to get rid of any air trapped between the sheets, preferably without the inclusion material flying out, then roll down firmly. Fold and twist the clay repeatedly to distribute the inclusion throughout the clay.

- **Embossing powder.** Mix it into translucent clay to tint it. The "tapestry" colors can produce the look of stone in a varied and manageable form. These homemade stone clays can even be used in caning, unlike commercial stone clays, which contain short fibers that catch on the edge of your blade and smear your cane.
- **Glitters.** Choose rubber-stamp glitters, which are more likely to be heat resistant than those from the stationery area. Test the glitter by mixing a bit into clay and baking it before you use it in a major project. A tiny touch of translucent microfine glitter is very effective. Thin sheets of the Fimo glitter clays can provide an attractive accent layer in caning.
- **Metal leaf.** Wad up and blend sheets of leaf into translucent clay to give it a soft sparkle. Use a layer next to a layer of translucent clay in mokumé gané for a lovely effect.
- **Dried aromatic herbs.** Mix them in to impart a scent that can last for months.
- **Partially baked clay.** Though it can't be restored to pliability, it can be chopped or grated and then sprinkled on or mixed into other colors.
- **Pearly Mylar flakes.** Otherwise known as artificial Christmas snow, pearly Mylar can be mixed into translucent clay with a trace of pink or turquoise clay to make faux opal. Use irregular shreds for the most realistic effect.

Artist's Tip: If you want to try mixing in chopped crayons, be sure to bake the clay on a thick pad of paper toweling set in a pan with a rim, to catch the wax as the crayons melt out during baking (the wax is flammable). The cavities left by the wax will be brilliantly colored by the crayon dye. Lindly Haunani, who pioneered this technique, also uses children's play sand as an inclusion; it will dull your blade, so reserve one for just this purpose.

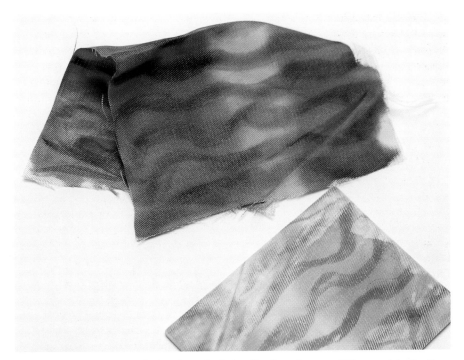

Use felt-tipped pens to create freehand transfer designs like these. See page 66 for complete directions.

Pigments

- **Acrylic paints.** Ordinary acrylic craft paints stick well to the clay surface; allow them to dry before covering with another layer of clay or the remaining water will turn into steam bubbles. Some artists use acrylics as a layer in mokumé gané.

- **Genesis brand polymer paints.** These paints have the handling qualities and transparency of oil paint but stay wet until set by heat.

- **Embossing powders.** These dry granules of plastic can be mixed into clay or used with glycerin-heavy embossing ink to coat the surface.

- **Rubber-stamp inks.** Crafter's inks will dry on wet clay, which can then be shaped and cut; once baked, the inks are permanent. Some permanent dye inks will mark baked clay.

- **Mica powders.** These now come in fabulous iridescent colors. They can be mixed into translucent clay or brushed onto the surface. Varnish a surface coat to keep it from rubbing off.

- **Oil paint.** In any quantity, oil paint will make solid polymer clay permanently sticky, though the tiniest amount can be smoothed harmlessly on the surface of a transfer image to tint it. But do use oil paints for tinting Liquid Sculpey (acrylics will make it foamy).

- **Artists' pastels.** Rub pastels on a piece of paper, then use a brush to lift the powder and apply it to polymer clay. Coat with varnish to prevent the pigment from rubbing off.

Safety Tip: To protect your lungs, always use a dust mask when working with powders, especially the metal pulvers. Dust masks can be found at any hardware store.

Metal Leafing and Tooling Foils

Gilding foil can be added to raw clay; it will stick directly. Composite leaf comes in brass, copper, aluminum, and multicolored brass (patterned or treated with heat or chemicals). Precious metal leafing such as silver and gold are also available. Leaf comes slipped between the pages of tissue-paper booklets. Open the booklet and lay the clay sheet right on the leaf; cut around it with a sharp craft knife. Burnish it down gently to get rid of bubbles. For a beautiful crackle effect, work it with your fingers or run it through the pasta machine on successively smaller settings from two different directions. For a pattern, press a deep-cut rubber stamp over the leaf, bake, then sand away the leaf from the raised areas. To keep it from tarnishing or rubbing off, protect it with varnish after baking.

Special foil designed for tooling can be incised with a ball-ended embossing tool, then covered with tinted Transparent Liquid Sculpey for a faux enamel effect; the wind chime project on page 62 will show you how.

Transfers

One delightful way to embellish the surface is to transfer an image or pattern to it. There are several ways to do this.

- **Photocopies.** Lay a dark black-and-white photocopy face down on a sheet of fresh, light-colored clay. Burnish it down with a bone folder or the back of a spoon to get rid of air pockets; it won't transfer where it doesn't touch. Leave it for about 20 minutes; warm it with your fingers if you like. The plasticizer in the clay will start to grab the toner in the copy. Bake it, then gently peel off the paper while it's quite hot. The toner should have transferred from the paper to the clay. Some brands of photocopiers don't make good transfers; older machines with fresh toner seem to work better. Test different machines until you find a good one. To help speed the toner transfer, try dabbing rubbing alcohol or gin on the back of the paper with a cotton swab. Or try leaving the paper on the raw clay overnight, baking, and soaking off the paper; you'll get raised lines like an engraving. If desired, color the photocopy first with artists' pencils or pastels—the color will transfer too.

- **Heat transfer paper.** For a color transfer from an inkjet printer, use Canon or Hewlett Packard T-shirt transfer paper. Burnish it down, bake it, and peel off the paper while it's still hot. For a transfer from a color copier, use Lazertran transfer paper.

- **Translucent Liquid Sculpey.** Coat a color or black-and-white photocopy, or a glossy image from a magazine page, with a thin layer of TLS, and bake according to the manufacturer's directions. Then peel the decal off the paper and apply to baked or raw clay that has been thinly coated with TLS; bake.

- **Prismacolor markers.** Cloth treated with these alcohol-based inks can be pressed into raw clay; apply alcohol to the back of the cloth to transfer the color. See the book covers project on page 66 for a full description.

Finishing Touches
Carving, Drilling, and Antiquing

Once fully baked, polymer clay can be easily carved, incised, filed, sawed, or drilled. Under-baked clay is usually too brittle to withstand this treatment. Experiment with wood-carving tools, sculpting tools, and any other kind of implement you can find at the art and craft supply store. Once carved, try rubbing acrylic paint into the grooves to accentuate them.

To drill a thin or small piece of polymer clay, mark the area first, and use a needle tool to gently dent the area. Then, simply hand-twist a drill bit into the dent to enlarge it. For thicker or larger pieces of clay, use a small hobby drill.

Artist's Tip: *Incised or cut areas will likely appear white, but this residue can be removed. Also, try re-baking the piece, if necessary.*

Polishing

Many of the projects in this book have been polished to create a glorious, glasslike finish. Polishing translucent clay is especially effective, because the transparency is greatly enhanced.

Polymer clay bakes to a pleasant matte surface, but if you sand and buff it, it will take a finish as smooth and glossy as a fine guitar; the metallic clays will glow, and the translucent ones will be almost as clear as glass. When working with wet/dry sandpaper, always use it in water (a bowlful will do it) to keep the clay cool and the dust out of the air and in the water, where you don't risk breathing it in. If you want to remove a lot of clay, start at 180 grit (fairly coarse), then progress to 320-, 400-, and 600-grit; if you want a real shine, get superfine paper (800- and 1,000-grit, on up) at the auto equipment shop. Finally, buff it until glossy on your jeans or other cotton cloth. Aficionados may want to polish with a bench grinder with an unstitched cotton wheel, or even a variable speed buffer made for jewelers. Buffing attachments are available for hobby drills.

Artist's Tip: *Keep the buffing wheel moving at all times. If you let it linger too long in one spot, the friction could damage the clay.*

See page 62 for directions on filling carved designs.

Transforming the Clay

Polymer clay can be combined with many other materials, but there are so many special clays—glittery, pearly, opaque, transparent—that it can also be completely transformed without using anything other than the clay! In this chapter, we'll explore how to manipulate this medium with astounding effects.

One satisfying basic way to transform polymer clay is to stack many thin layers of contrasting colors and roll it into beautiful canes. The resulting "jelly-roll" canes can be further shaped, then sliced to create gorgeous veneers and beads. This technique can be varied in so many ways—and each one is sure to be original. It's a great introduction to caning.

You'll also discover the fascinating attributes of metallic clay, which contains particles of a shimmery mineral called mica. By simply rolling mica-rich clay repeatedly, you can actually change the alignment of the particles. We'll show you how to use this technique to create a stunning holographic "ghost" image.

Another basic technique is to blend clay colors. Clays can be blended to make smooth gradations from one hue to another, then stacked and recombined to create stripes, plaids, and other patterns. We'll teach you how to elaborate and expand on this technique to create visually intricate patterns using a pasta machine attachment and contrasting clay colors.

With the array of available colors, and more specialty clays arriving on the market all the time, there's no end to the effects you can create using only clay. Experiment—you're sure to get results no one else has ever seen.

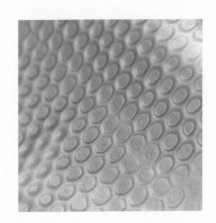

Chrysanthemum Cane Heart Pendants

These heart-shaped pendants are covered with chrysanthemum-shaped slices of a beautiful, simple, and versatile translucent polymer clay cane. Transform a basic jelly-roll cane using a simple distortion technique, then use thin slices to decorate polymer clay heart pendants. Once you have mastered this technique, you can move on to cover other things—frames, light switch plates, sculptures, glassware, pottery. Don't worry about cutting the cane into perfectly even slices. Slight variations in thickness result in a more interesting, variegated effect. Slicing the cane diagonally helps to create an even greater illusion of depth.

Artist: Elissa Powell

Materials

- basic polymer clay equipment and supplies (see page 10)
- ½ block of white clay
- 1 block of pearl clay
- 1 block of translucent clay
- scrap clay for the core of the pendants
- ¼ block of brightly colored base clay to cover the core of the pendants
- screw eye
- varnish, if desired
- pasta machine
- credit card or similar stiff, thin object
- cellophane or plastic wrap
- small piece of cardstock or a matchbook cover
- soft cloth

Getting Started

Choose the base color of the pendant carefully. When slices from the same cane are applied over different colors, the final results can vary greatly.

1 Make the cane.

Roll the white clay through the pasta machine on the next-to-thinnest setting. Trim the clay so that the sheet is about 10" (25 cm) long and 4" to 5" (10 cm to 13 cm) wide. Roll the pearl clay through the pasta machine on the thickest setting, then do the same with the translucent clay. Trim both sheets so that they're the same size as the white sheet. Lay the pearl clay on top of the white clay, then lay the translucent clay on top of the pearl clay. Smooth the stack with a roller to get rid of any air bubbles. Trim one of the shorter edges to make it straight. Run the roller across the edge to bevel the layers, then roll the sheets up tightly. This creates a basic jelly roll cane.

Cover one edge of the credit card or similar stiff, thin object with cellophane or plastic wrap. Gently and evenly press the covered edge of the credit card into the cane lengthwise. Roll the cane a quarter turn, then press the credit card into the clay again. Repeat twice more so that the cane has four evenly spaced indentations. Repeat the process four more times, pressing the credit card into the clay between each of the four original indentations. The cane should have eight deep, evenly spaced indentations. Allow the clay to rest at least 30 minutes to firm up, then trim off the rough edges at a slight angle.

TIP

Distort the cane immediately after making the jelly roll while the clay is still soft, warm, and pliable.

2 Prepare the heart cores.

Form the scrap clay into two balls, each about 1" (3 cm) in diameter. The scrap clay should be well blended so that no lumps remain. Roll the brightly colored base clay through the pasta machine on a thin setting, then wrap it around the cores to create an attractive, uniform color. Remove any excess clay, and smooth the surface of the covered cores.

3 Decorate the cores.

Slice the end of the chrysanthemum cane at a slight angle, then cut several slices as thin as possible; however, don't worry about cutting the cane into perfectly even slices: Slight variations in thickness result in a more interesting, variegated effect. Roll a few slices through the pasta machine on medium-thin setting, then place them on the balls of clay, overlapping the edges. (This step enhances the visual depth created when translucent and opaque clays are used together.) When the balls are completely covered, roll them gently to smooth and round them out.

4 Shape and finish the hearts.

Examine the balls of cane-covered clay to choose the fronts and tops of the hearts. Form the point at the bottom of the heart by rolling an area of the clay ball tightly between your fingers. The clay should resemble an upside-down tear drop. Form the upper lobes of a heart by making an indentation in the middle of the rounded part of the tear drop. To deepen and accentuate the cleft, press a folded piece of cardstock, such as a business card, between the lobes, and rock it back and forth. Smooth and refine the shape as desired.

Now you're ready to insert the screw eye so you can hang the heart. Make a pilot hole about ½" (1 cm) deep exactly between the two lobes with a needle tool, then enlarge the hole slightly using a tiny circular motion. Insert the needle into the hole about ¼" (6 mm) deep, and press sideways with the end of the needle on each side of the pilot hole to create slits to accommodate the sides of the screw eye. (Creating side slits will prevent any distortion caused by pressing the screw eye downward.) Carefully insert the screw eye, making sure that it's perfectly parallel with the plane of the heart, and pinch closed the open spaces around it. If it's at all crooked, gently twist it into proper alignment with some tweezers or needle nose pliers. Bake following the clay manufacturer's directions.

To achieve the ultimate transparent effect, there are no shortcuts. Sand the baked hearts, first with 400-grit wet/dry sandpaper, then with 800-grit (or finer) sandpaper. Buff with a soft cloth until shiny. Finally, apply a coat of varnish, if desired.

Variations

Adding inclusions—such as glitter, sand, embossing powders, and dried herbs—into polymer clay is a simple and satisfying way to embellish a project. The technique produces especially striking effects when applied to translucent clay. You can use Fimo glitter clay for one of your layers, or you can make your own glitter clay: First pour some glitter into a bowl. Next, flatten conditioned clay into a pancake, and press it into the glitter. Then, fold the pancake in half, with the glitter on the inside; pinch the sides shut to keep the glitter from flying out, flatten the clay, and roll it into a log. Twist, flatten, fold, and roll the clay again. Repeat these steps until the glitter is evenly mixed throughout the clay. This technique can be used to mix other inclusions into clay, but make sure that all materials are completely dry. You can also use metal leaf as one of the layers in creating the cane, sprinkle multicolored shreds of clay on one of the layers to give a confetti look, or substitute a multicolored blend for the white layer.

Instead of distorting the spiral into the chrysanthemum form, use it as is or square it off. Try covering your cores with other decorative clay, such as mokumé gané (see page 36) or metallic "ghost image" clay (see page 26).

Textured Ikebana Vase

Artist: Mona Kissel

Ikebana, the elegant Japanese art of flower arranging, calls for an equally elegant vase. The beautiful finish on this one is created by imprinting a pearly or metallic clay slab with a textured surface, slicing off the top layer of the texture, rolling it smooth, and then polishing the baked piece to a high shine. This technique produces an almost holographic effect sometimes called a ghost image—that is, a pattern you can see but can't feel. One to three flowers can be displayed in this vase. Use it with a pin frog, which will support the flowers easily. Simply add water every other day, and the flowers can be enjoyed for up to two weeks. Pin frogs are available at craft and floral supply stores.

Materials

- basic polymer clay equipment and supplies (see page 10)
- 1 block of black clay, Premo
- 3 blocks of gold clay, Premo
- 1 ⅛" (about 3 cm) round floral pin frog
- 1 ¼" (3 cm) round biscuit or cookie cutter
- small square Plexiglas sheet
- pasta machine
- Shade Tex brand textured plastic sheets for imprinting, cut to 4" x 5" (10 cm x 13 cm)
- spray bottle
- bowl with warm soapy water
- buffer or bench grinder with unstitched cotton polishing wheel
- small dab of candle adhesive or floral clay

Getting Started

Many kinds of textured sheets, found objects, and tools, including mounted or unmounted rubber stamps, can be used to imprint the clay for this project. Shade Tex sheets with a hexagonal pattern were used to make this vase.

1 Make the base of the vase.

(Indented Ball) Roll a ball of black clay slightly larger than the diameter of the pin frog. Press a round-ended object such as a brayer handle about three-quarters of the way down into the ball, leaving the bottom of the base at least ¼" (5 mm) thick.

(Vase) Next, form the walls around the depression by stretching the clay upward. The walls should be about ¼" (5 mm) thick and slightly higher than the pin frog. Press the pin frog into the bottom of the base so the pin frog will fit securely once baked. Make sure the bottom of the base is at least ⅛" (3 mm) thick and the hole's diameter is bigger than the 1 ¼" (3 cm) round cutter; if necessary, stretch it a bit. Remove the pin frog. Then place waxed paper on top of and underneath the base. Use a square Plexiglas sheet to flatten the clay and ensure that the vase will be level. Bake the base at 275° F (135° C) for 30 minutes, then allow it to cool and harden.

(Vase with clay log on top) Roll a ¼" (6 mm) thick log of soft, tacky black clay that's long enough to make a ring around the top edge of the base. Press the log gently into place and set the base aside.

TIP

Always use clean waxed paper for different stages of the project to prevents nicks, fingerprints, and other damage to the clay. This will reduce the amount of sanding time necessary to achieve the high-gloss finish.

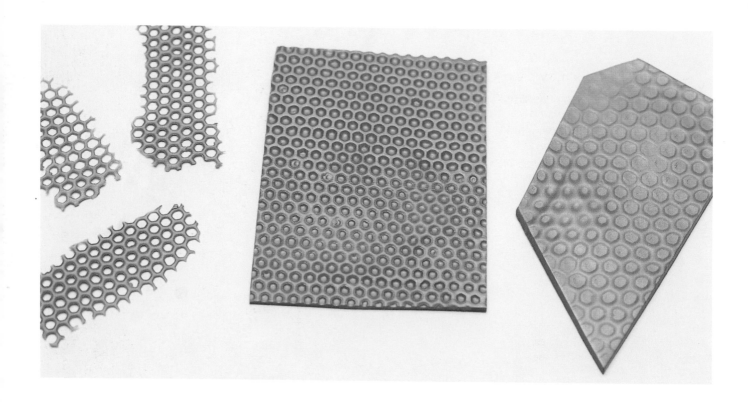

2 Make the top of the vase.

Fold the gold clay, then roll it through the pasta machine on the thickest setting 15 to 20 times, to align the reflective mica particles and bring them to the surface. Then divide the gold sheet of clay into 5 even parts.

To imprint the "ghost image" on the clay, roll 1 of the 5 parts through the pasta machine on the thickest setting. Trim the sheet so it's about 4" x 5" (10 cm x 13 cm), and lay it on a paper towel. Use a spray bottle to moisten the surface with water, which will keep the clay from sticking to your texture sheet. Place a texture sheet on the clay, and roll both through the pasta machine on the thickest setting. Next, gently remove the texture sheet, and place the imprinted clay on a piece of waxed paper. Blot the clay dry with paper towel, and trim any rough edges. Also dry the pasta machine. Allow the clay to stand for one hour, then remove it from the waxed paper, and press it gently on a plastic cutting board or a sheet of poster board, making sure it sticks to the board.

Using a flexible tissue blade, slice away long, paper-thin strips of the textured clay until all raised surfaces have been skimmed off. These pieces can be flipped over and recycled for use in another project.

Then roll another piece of gold clay through the pasta machine on a fairly thin setting. Place this sheet under the imprinted one, and roll gently over the surface with a brayer. Roll the combined sheets through the pasta machine on the thickest setting. Repeat this procedure with another piece of gold clay to completely flatten the imprinted surface.

Stack the remaining two pieces of clay, and roll them through the pasta machine on the thickest setting. Lay this sheet on waxed paper, then place the imprinted sheet on top of it. Roll firmly and evenly over the surface of the clay with a brayer. The multilayered clay sheet should be about ¼" (6 mm) thick. Trim the edges with a tissue blade to create a four-sided shape, although not necessarily a rectangle. Then cut a hole in the center using a 1 ¼" (3 cm) round biscuit or cookie cutter.

3 Assemble and finish the vase.

Lay the vase top face-down on a new piece of waxed paper. Turn the base upside down, and position it over the hole in the vase top. If the log on the top of the vase has stiffened, condition it again until tacky. Use the Plexiglas square to gently press the base to the vase top. Turn the vase over so that it's facing up, then set it on a piece of clean waxed paper. Remove the protective waxed paper from the vase top, and apply it again. Use the Plexiglas square again to gently press the top to the base. Smooth the corners of the vase top down through the waxed paper so they touch the work surface. This will ensure a steady, stable vase. Bake at 275° F (135° C) for 60 minutes.

To bring out the chatoyant, three-dimensional ghost image effect of the imprinted texture, sand the vase top in a bowl of warm, soapy water with successively finer grits of wet/dry sandpaper (400-, 600-, 800-, 1,500-, and then 2,000-grit). Wash the vase in clean, warm, soapy water, then dry it. Use a cotton-polishing wheel to buff the piece, then wash and dry it again. Finally, apply a small dab of candle adhesive or floral clay to bottom of pin frog to secure it in the bottom of the vase.

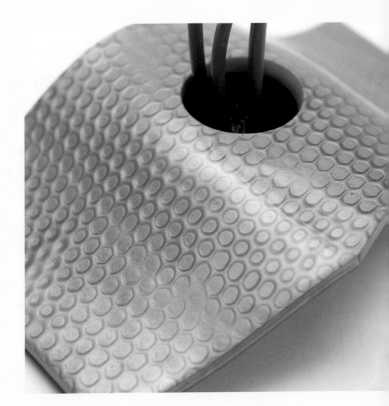

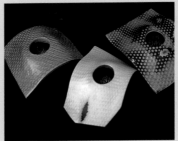

Variations

The graceful, simple form of these vases is the perfect canvas for experimenting with texture and color. Try simulating nature: wood, water, stones, foliage—these patterns will complement any flower. Specialty texturing tools are commercially available, but experimenting with found metal or plastic objects like screens or grids can lead to great discoveries. Also try creating a texture that can be felt as well as seen—use rubber stamps, carving gouges, or custom-made clay tools.

"Ghost image" clay can be used for many other projects, from bracelets to pins to picture frames.

Faux-Fabric Poof Box

Artist: Susan Hy...

Shows and conferences often inspire clay lovers to create novel techniques. One theme at the second Ravensdale conference—held near Seattle roughly every three years—was "Reinventing the Box." Inspired by this theme, artist Susan Hyde created this poof box, which features a faux-fabric technique. She combined the streaky blend technique invented by Judith Skinner and Kathleen Amt and added her own special touch: the linguini effect. Use contrasting shreds of clay and embossing powder for further effect, make it into a cane or loaf, fold a sheet into a curvy box, and get sealed-in air to support the baking form.

Materials

- basic polymer clay equipment and supplies (see page 10)
- cardstock or large index card
- Transparent Liquid Sculpey (TLS)
- the equivalent of 2 to 3 blocks of Premo clay in metallic blue, cadmium red, ecru, turquoise, fuschia, and gold
- embossing powder or superfine glitter in a contrasting color
- handkerchief-size piece of fine cotton fabric
- pasta machine with linguini attachment
- ruler
- small straw, such as a coffee stirrer

Getting Started

For this project, the clay doesn't need to be conditioned in advance—it will be conditioned by the process of making the blend.

1 Make a six-color streaky blend.

Make a cardstock triangle template about 6" (15 cm) long and a bit less than 2" (5 cm) wide. Set your pasta machine on the thickest setting, and roll out a sheet of each color. Fold the sheets on the diagonal to make a double thickness of clay. With the craft knife, cut triangles from the double layers. Arrange the double-layer triangles head-to-foot to form a rectangle. Use half-triangles on the sides. Roll with the brayer, and press together with your fingers. Run this clay sheet through the pasta machine five times on the thickest setting, folding it in half across the "grain" each time and sending it through the machine fold first. Never fold it lengthwise before running it through the pasta machine or the blend will become muddy.

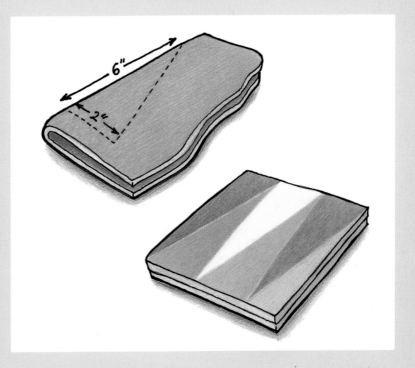

2 Add inclusions to the blend.

Sprinkle about a tablespoonful of embossing powder or superfine glitter on half of the clay sheet, fold it over, and pinch the sides to keep the slippery embossing powder from scattering; press down gently to join the halves. Run the clay through the pasta machine fold first; fold again, and repeat 10 times. You now have a streaky color blend. Trim it into a long rectangle.

3 Add contrasting linguini shreds to the blend.

Sprinkle a little baby powder on the surface of three 2" (5 cm) strips of unconditioned clay in bright colors that contrast, or even clash, with the streaky blended sheet. Spread the powder all over. Make "worms" from the bright clay by running through the linguini attachment of the pasta machine. If you don't have a linguini attachment, use a ruler and a sharp craft knife to produce plenty of linguini-size shreds. Place them on one end of the blended clay sheet; they'll become colorful speckles in the final piece. Fold the slab across the middle, run it through the pasta machine again, and repeat.

(1)

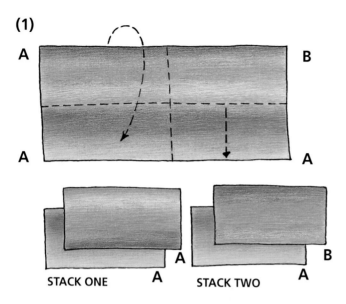

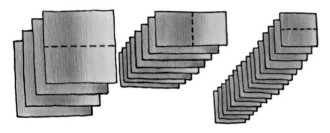

STACK ONE   A   STACK TWO   A

(2) FOR STRIPES:

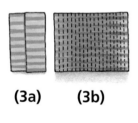

FOR PLAIDS:

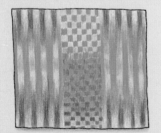
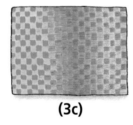

(3a)   **(3b)**   **(3c)**

4 **Make striped and plaid clay stacks.**

Cut the clay sheet in half across the middle. Take one part, cut it in half in the direction of the streaks, and flip the halves together, fronts facing. This is stack one. Repeat with the other part, and place one half on top of the other without turning or flipping it so that the bottom of one side rests on the top of the other side. This is stack two. When you have finished, stack one will make a striped pattern and stack two a plaid pattern.

For stripes, slice stack one in half, across the streaks, and stack again. (See diagram 1.) Repeat twice so you have a little loaf with horizontal layers, like a club sandwich or layer cake. (See diagram 2.) Slice down the side to produce a striped piece.

For plaids, slice stack two in half, across the streaks, and stack again. Repeat twice, as you did for the striped stack. Then, tip the loaf over on its side so the layers are standing up and running straight toward you. Mark it in regular increments about ¼" (6 mm) apart, and slice it, cutting downward perpendicular to the layers. Separate the slices a little, and turn every other one around so the blends don't match. (See diagram 3a.) Pack and trim the stack into a neat loaf. The top will have a plaid pattern. (See diagram 3b).

When your "fabric" loaves are finished, cut several thin slices of each, giving you stripes and plaid. Roll out a thin sheet of any conditioned clay (it won't show once the project is complete). Patch the fabric slices together on this backing sheet in a pleasing pattern. Run each patchwork sheet through the pasta machine repeatedly, starting at the thickest setting and stepping down to setting #4 or #5. Before each rolling, rotate the sheet one turn so it doesn't stretch too far in one direction. The "cloth" will become quite thin and the pattern will expand. (See diagram 3c.)

5 **Make and laminate the poof box.**

Roll scrap clay through the pasta machine on the thickest setting to make about a 6" (15 cm) square. Place a layer of your patchwork faux fabric over it. Cover it with waxed paper, and roll it down firmly with the brayer to fuse the layers. Cut out a circle of your faux fabric about 4" (10 cm) across. Turn the square over, place the circle in the center, and roll it down. This becomes the inside of the box and will be beautiful when you look inside.

Place the square between two pieces of cloth and roll hard again with your brayer to fuse the clay layers and give the box a nice cloth texture. Trim the square with a ruler and sharp craft knife to bevel the edges toward the inside of the box.

7 Make the poof box lid.

Remove the box from the oven, and let it cool just until you can handle it. Take your sharp craft knife and, holding it at an angle as if you were cutting the lid of a jack o'lantern, cut a square top from the box. You can follow the fabric patterns in the clay if you like. Cut on an angle that slopes in toward the center of the box. If you cut straight down, there won't be a ledge for the lid to sit on and it will fall straight down into the box. If you like, cover the bottom of the lid with a patch of faux fabric, because it's usually pretty messy from all the pinching and not symmetrical. Trim the patch even with the slope of the lid, and bake for 10 minutes, just to harden the clay. For the handle on top that will never come off, use a cane slice or any attractive piece of clay. Add it to a disk of unbaked clay (to make the surface smoother), dab on some TLS, press it onto the top, and bake for 20 minutes.

6 Inflate the poof box.

With the circle facing up, lift up two adjacent corners of the square, put the corners together, and gently squeeze the edges together. Bring up another corner and finally the fourth. It can be tricky to get the edges stuck together neatly. Alternatively, you can pinch them upward like a ruffled pie crust edge. When all the edges are stuck together, poke the straw into the little hole in the top where the points meet, and blow so the box inflates. Remove the straw, pinch the hole closed, and quickly get the box into the oven. The air inside will keep the box inflated. Bake 30 to 45 minutes at 275° F (135° C).

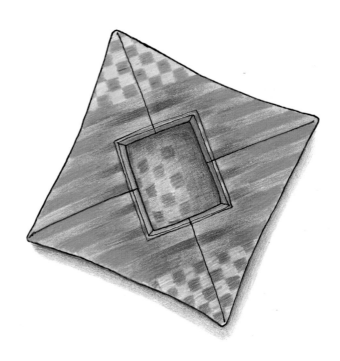

Variations

Faux fabric can be used anywhere patterned or decorated clay is wanted, from an ikebana vase top (see page 26) to a fitted box (see page 44).

Experiment with different kinds of shreds using a clay extruder with various attachments. Imagine making faux-fabric accents for clay figures, dolls, or other sculptures! Be sure to see page 40 for tips and inspiration.

Creating the Structure

One of the most satisfying things you can make with polymer clay is a three-dimensional piece. As with all modeling media, sound structural techniques are integral to using polymer clay effectively, especially when making functional pieces—you don't want your creations to fall apart! In this chapter, you'll discover some of the many ways to create lovely, durable artwork.

One simple technique is to cover a form with thin veneers of clay. Glass, plain metal, and papier mâché are good candidates. If a rounded form is enclosed, no glue is needed. If the object has straight sides, you can coat it with white PVA glue and let that dry. Then add the clay, which will stick to the dry glue. This makes it possible to create vessels of nearly any shape. Use veneers with at least some translucent clay for candleholders that diffuse light beautifully. Also try encasing cardboard pieces, like the matchbox used for the Storyteller Doll on page 40.

You'll also discover the secret to making a perfect round box using an ordinary mailing tube. By layering sheets of clay around a cardboard cylinder, you'll be able to make a box with a top that fits so well, it will make a popping sound when you open it! Another technique you'll learn is how to make extraordinarily thin but strong polymer clay leaves that can be wired and used to build a lush centerpiece like the one on page 48. Made with a special clay mixture and reinforced with flexible varnish, the leaves can be handled and manipulated with ease.

Remember, the methods we explore in this chapter can be used to create new projects with just a little modification. Just follow the basic technique, and add your own special touch.

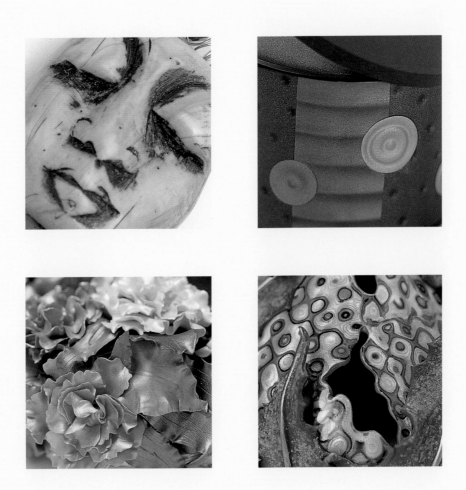

Leafy Mokumé Gané Vessel

Mokumé gané is a traditional Japanese metal-working technique used to create gorgeous, intricate patterns. Because the technique involves stacking thin layers, it can be easily adapted to polymer clay. Unlimited patterns of mokumé gané are possible, so experiment with different clay colors, tools, and materials, such as metal leaf or inclusions. A ripple blade is used in this project to create the dotted pattern. Use Premo-brand clay to reproduce the brilliant pearlescent sheen of this vessel. To make a lovely and functional candleholder, use tinted translucent clays or a mix of opaque and translucent clays.

Artist: Jody Bishel

Materials

- basic polymer clay equipment and supplies (see page 10)
- 1 ⅜ blocks of gold clay, Premo
- ⅛ block of copper clay, Premo
- ⅛ block of burnt umber clay, Premo
- ⅜ block of black clay, Premo
- ¼ block of silver clay, Premo
- squared-up lump of scrap clay
- 4" (10 cm) round glass vessel

- glossy polymer-clay-compatible varnish, such as Flecto Varathane Elite Diamond ISP
- Translucent Liquid Sculpey (TLS) or Sculpey Diluent
- copper-colored mica powder, such as Pearl Ex
- pasta machine
- ripple blade
- flat brush
- small round paintbrush

Getting Started

Ripple blades tend to catch more debris along the edge than straight blades, so clean as needed by wiping carefully with isopropyl alcohol on a paper towel. Painting the unsharpened edge of the ripple blade with bright nail polish will make it easier to avoid picking up the wrong side and cutting yourself.

1 Make the mokumé gané veneer.

Begin by rolling two separate sheets of marbled clay through a pasta machine on the thickest setting. For sheet A, marble together ⅜ block of gold clay, the copper clay, and the burnt umber clay. For sheet B, marble together the black and silver clay.

Cut both sheets into 1½" (4 cm) squares, and stack them to form a loaf. Alternate between sheets A and B. Then, roll gently over the surface to eliminate air bubbles and adhere the layers to each other. Press an edge of the loaf into the lump of scrap clay so the layers are vertical. Using the ripple blade, cut ⅛" (3 mm) thick slices. Try to make each slice of the same thickness. The scrap clay will hold the loaf steady while cutting. Then, roll the slices through the pasta machine at the thickest setting, just enough to flatten them. Mix up the order of the sheets, then stack them again. The edges should be aligned so that two sides are wavy and the other two are straight. Again, roll gently over the surface. Next, press one of the straight edges of the loaf to the scrap clay. Using the ripple blade, cut ⅛" (3 mm) thick slices. The slices should reveal a dot pattern. If there are no dots, give the loaf a quarter turn, then cut again. Roll the slices through the pasta machine on the thickest setting, then roll the slices through again, one setting above the thickest. Continue rolling the slices through on successively thinner settings, stopping at setting #4. Give the slices a quarter turn between each rolling to keep the dots round and to avoid stretching out the pattern too much in one direction.

2 Cover the glass vessel.

Place the slices over the outside of the glass votive. Piece them together so that the edges meet; don't overlap them, which will create raised seams. Roll gently over the edges to smooth and fuse the seams. Bake the votive for 20 minutes at 275° F (135° C). Once the vessel has cooled, wet-sand the clay with 400-grit sandpaper, then 600-grit sandpaper to refine the surface and remove any imperfections. Use a flat brush to apply two coats of glossy polymer clay-compatible varnish, such as Flecto Varathane Elite Diamond ISP, then allow the vessel to dry completely.

3 Make and attach the leaves to the vessel.

Roll the remaining block of gold clay through the pasta machine on setting #4. Fold the sheet in half, and roll it though again. Keep repeating the process to brighten and intensify the metallic sheen. Be sure to make the sheet as wide as the pasta machine will allow. Then, cut five 2" (5 cm) wide strips from the sheet. Fold the strips lengthwise, and press gently, then open the strips. This will create a groove down the center of the strips. Next, cut out leaf shapes with the groove in the center. Flatten and smooth the edges of the leaves for a more realistic look. Use a clean scrap of paper over the clay to avoid leaving fingerprints. The edges of the leaves can be ruffled by gently stretching the area. Curl the point of the leaves gently, if desired.

To attach the leaves to the votive, first use a craft knife to scratch the areas on the vessel where the leaves will be attached—underneath the vessel and at the lip. Dab the scratched areas with TLS or Sculpey Diluent. Then, press the base of each leaf onto the moistened clay underneath the vessel, then attach the top to the corresponding area at the lip of the vessel. The leaves will look especially graceful if they arch away from the sides of the vessel, as shown on facing page. Bake the vessel again for 30 minutes at 275° F (135° C).

4 Finish the leafy vessel.

Wipe the leaves with an isopropyl alcohol-soaked paper towel to remove any oils. Then, mix the copper-colored mica powder into a small amount of varnish. Use a small round brush to paint an accent stripe down the groove in the center of each leaf. Let dry. Use a flat brush to apply one or two coats of varnish to the leaves.

Variations

Try varying the shapes of the leaves, using more of them, and arranging them less regularly. Also try using other glass forms, from vases to hurricane lantern chimneys.

Mokumé gané is an intriguing technique with infinite variations. To make a simple, versatile block, layer alternating sheets of clay and metal leaf. Try using heat-treated leaf, which has beautiful color variegations. And be sure to use at least some translucent clay, which will create visual depth and allow the metal leaf in the block to show through the layers. Then experiment with translucent slices over a base of contrasting color. Sand, then buff to a high shine for the most stunning effects.

Storyteller Doll

This storyteller contains a hidden compartment, which opens to reveal an accordion-folded book. An ordinary matchbox serves as the structure for the compartment, demonstrating how everyday materials can be readily integrated with polymer clay. The book pages can be decorated with any number of things—a favorite quote written in calligraphy, rubber stamping, drawings that tell a tale, or a collage of inspiring images. The simple structural techniques described here can be easily adapted to create a doll with personal or cultural significance.

Artist: Dayle Doroshow

Materials

- basic polymer clay equipment and supplies (see page 10)
- ½ block of clay for head
- acrylic paint
- 1 block of clay for body
- slices of millefiore cane slices, mokumé gané slices, or other surface embellishments
- small cardboard matchbox
- decorative paper
- elastic cord
- wire and beads for headdress
- 2" (5 cm) eye pin

Getting Started

The face of this doll was sculpted by hand. Push molds can also be used; they can be handmade or purchased and are available in various styles and expressions.

1 Make the doll's head and body.

The doll's head can be sculpted from an elongated ball of clay, using a thumbnail to create the eyes, a needle tool to create the mouth, and a small snake of clay to create the nose. Once the face is formed, coat 1" (3 cm) of a 2" (5 cm) eye pin with glue, starting at the looped end. Insert the eye pin, loop first, 1" (3 cm) into the head. Bake following the manufacturer's directions. Once cool, rub acrylic paint over the face, then wipe away the excess so the features are highlighted.

To form the body, roll a large ball of clay into a fat log. Taper the log into a cone shape, then flatten it with a brayer until it's about ½" (1 cm) thick. The body can be decorated with millefiore cane slices, mokumé gané slices, or any other surface embellishments. To add millefiore inlays, place thin cane slices on the log before tapering it, then roll the log to adhere the slices.

2 Make the book holder and pages.

Place the outside sleeve of a cardboard matchbox on the doll's body, aligning the top edges of each, and mark where the bottom edge of the matchbox meets the clay. Then, flatten this area of the clay until it's about ⅛" (3 mm) thick, first with your hand and then with a brayer. Make sure the clay extends past the sides of the body to create flaps. Next, press the matchbox sleeve into the flattened area of the body, and fold the side flaps of clay up the sides of the matchbox. Trim the excess clay.

To make the book, accordion-fold a piece of paper that has been cut to the height of the matchbox. Decorate the pages as desired. Then, cut the matchbox open on the right side, along the creased edge. Glue the first "page" of the folded paper to the back of the matchbox. Decorate the front of the matchbox with paper, or paint it. To make a closure for the book, poke a hole through the cover and right side of the box. Thread a looped elastic cord through the side hole, and knot it. Then, wire a bead through the cover hole. To close the book, slip the elastic loop over the bead.

3 Assemble the doll.

Coat the remaining 1" (3 cm) of the eye pin that extends from the baked head with glue. Then insert the head into ⅛" (3 mm) of clay behind the matchbox. Bake following the clay manufacturer's directions.

4 Add accents.

Use beads, wire, charms, and any other desired materials to embellish the storyteller. The coiled headdress here was made by wrapping delicate wire around a knitting needle.

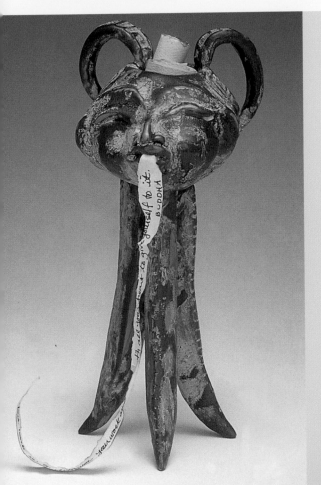

Variations

The basic technique of enclosing a box within polymer clay has limitless applications. Try enclosing a wooden container, perhaps with a sliding top, to create a treasure keeper. Or build a figurine and give it a small glass bottle to hold; then, fill the bottle with scented oil or a fragrant herbal sprig.

Another option is to custom-make a box. Sketch out a template, using a real box as a guide if desired, then use cardstock or cardboard to construct it. See the *Laminated Boxes* project on page 70 for more information on constructing oven-safe paper containers.

Fitted Jewelry Box

Artist: Dan Cormier

Over the past several years, I've made various wearable vessels and small boxes with precisely fitted lids that often pop when you open them. I developed my own techniques for building these containers, and though I've made them in all sorts of shapes and sizes, they all rely on the same principle—using paper as a release to prevent two layers of clay from sticking. A form provides the initial shape, but each layer of clay becomes the form for the layer that follows. This jewelry box will teach you the basic steps, and when you're done, you'll have a place to keep some of your wearable polymer clay jewelry creations.

Materials

- basic polymer clay equipment and supplies (see page 10)
- several sheets of standard copy paper
- disappearing-color glue stick (colored when wet, dries clear)
- 2 pieces of 100% cotton rag paper or tracing paper, 4" x 12" (10 cm x 30 cm) and 2" x 12" (5 cm x 30 cm)
- cardboard postal tube, 2 ½" (6 cm) diameter, 6" (15 cm) length
- 4 blocks of clay, any brand and color, for the base of box
- cellophane tape
- 2 blocks of clay, any brand and color, for decorative veneer
- pasta machine
- flat-topped plastic bead vials in various heights
- Plexiglas rod

Getting Started

Before baking, some clays adhere to rag paper (and baked clay) better than others. If you have trouble, take some scrap clay and rub it over the surface you're trying to adhere to, just enough to create a "glue." This should help the next layer stick.

1 Wrap the tube with paper.

Lay a piece of copy paper on the work surface. Then, using the glue stick, apply glue along one of the shorter edges of the 4" x 12" (10 cm x 30 cm) piece of rag paper. The coat of glue should be ½" (1 cm) wide and should completely cover the area. Next, lay the cardboard tube over the unglued short edge of the paper, and begin rolling it around the tube until the paper attaches to itself. Be careful not to adhere the paper to the tube. Make sure the paper fits snugly around the tube, but still slides freely.

2 Make the base of the box.

Using your Plexiglas rod and pasta machine, prepare a sheet of clay about 3" x 10" (8 cm x 25 cm) (rough edges are okay at this point). Use the third-thickest setting. For example, if #1 is your thickest, use setting #3. Place your clay sheet on a sheet of office paper; working on paper will allow you to move and lift the clay easily. With your ruler and craft knife, cut a clean edge along one of the short ends of the clay sheet. Reposition your clay sheet so the cut edge is about ¼" (6 mm) away from and parallel to the edge of your paper; turn it so the cut edge is closest to you. Place the paper-covered tube on the clay sheet.

Use the work-surface paper to lift the clay sheet and gently press it against the tube. Apply only as much pressure as you need to release the clay from your work-surface paper and adhere it to the rag paper on the tube. Try not to distort or flatten the clean edge of the clay sheet. Start in the center and work out toward the ends until the clay sheet is attached to the rag paper. Continue rolling the sheet around the tube.

To preserve the clay's uniform thickness, don't let the ends overlap. Use the first cut edge as a guide to trim the clay sheet. When the clay sheet has almost wrapped the tube, gently roll the cut edge onto the sheet to mark it, making sure to extend the lines past the edges of the clay; this will be your trim line. Unroll the cut edge of the clay, then roll the rough edge over the marked area and trim. Set the excess trimmed clay aside. The clay sheet is now exactly the right size to fit the tube.

To seal the seam, gently support your clay-covered tube in one hand, and push one cut edge toward the other with your thumb so they stick together. Again, start in the center and work out to each end until the cut edges are sealed. By starting in the middle, you will get a clean seal and a snug wrap, and you will avoid trapping air between the clay and the rag paper. To smooth the outer surface of the clay and fully adhere it to the rag paper, wrap the clay-covered tube snugly in a sheet of copy paper, and roll it on your work surface. Tack the paper together with a little tape.

Now, trim the top and bottom of the clay. For this jewelry box, you'll need a cylinder 2½" (6 cm) long. Using a ruler and the end of your blade, mark the places where you want to make your cuts. Stand the tube up on the factory-cut end. Trimming the cylinder evenly is a bit tricky, so you'll use a plastic bead vial to create a platform supporting and steadying your blade. Stand a vial next to the tube, and lay your blade flat on the lid of the vial, with the cutting edge toward the tube. Slide the covering paper up or down the tube until one of your marks is in line with the blade. Hold the blade in place on the vial with one hand, and slide the tube over to the blade with the other. When the blade has cut into the clay sheet, rotate the tube to cut around the full circumference of the cylinder. To cut the other end of your box cylinder, remove the tape, reposition the clay and paper wrap along the tube, and repeat the rotating cut. Use a taller vial if necessary. Peel the excess clay off the tube, leaving a cleanly trimmed 2½" (6 cm) cylinder. Stand the tube on a baking tray, and bake according to the manufacturer's directions. Let the cylinder cool on the tube before continuing.

3 Make the lid of the box.

To make the lid, you will use the 2" x 12" (5 cm x 30 cm) piece of rag paper. Your clay sheet should be about 2" x 10" (5 cm x 25 cm). I used a different color. Repeat the first two steps, but over the baked clay now surrounding your tube. First, prepare the rag paper with glue and wrap it around the tube-and-clay form, making sure the rag paper is snug but moves freely over the baked layer. Then, wrap the rag paper with the new clay sheet, making sure the new clay layer is centered on the rag paper wrap and snug and the seam is sealed; the new clay shouldn't overlap or touch the baked clay beneath. Remember to smooth and adhere the clay fully by rolling it within a copy paper wrap. Trim the new clay cylinder to 1" (3 cm) long. Bake, and cool.

Now, release the clay cylinders by gently twisting and sliding them off the postal tube. The rag paper will enable them to separate easily. Remove the paper from both layers. The second, shorter layer will be larger in diameter than the other, and the first clay layer will nest snugly within it.

4 Make the top and bottom of the box.

Using the same setting on the pasta machine, prepare two small sheets of clay.

To make the top for the lid of the box, place one of the clay sheets on a piece of paper. Place the box lid on the clay sheet, and gently press it in place, without pushing it into the clay. With your blade, trim around the contour of the lid until all excess clay is removed. Carefully lift the lid from the work surface, and gently press the fresh clay with your fingers to secure it to the baked clay edge. This will ensure it adheres during baking. Repeat these steps to make the bottom for your base. Stand the lid and base, open ends facing up, on your baking tray. Bake and cool. You have completed a basic box.

5 Create a flush lid.

At this point, the box lid overlaps the base, like an ice cream carton. But in the finished jewelry box, the lid will be flush with the base. To create this we must add another layer of clay to most of the base.

First, prepare a sheet of clay about 3" x 10" (8 cm x 25 cm). You will use this clay sheet to wrap the base as in step 3, but because you want these clay layers to adhere, there's no rag paper buffer. Wrap the new clay around the base, and trim it top and bottom using the baked clay edges beneath to guide your blade. Now, using a vial to steady and support your blade, trim away about ½" (1 cm) of clay from the top (open) edge of the base. Stand the base on a tray, open end up, and bake. You now have a box with a lid that slips over the lining of the base and rests on the edge of the layer you have just added, creating a uniform outer layer.

6 Decorate the box.

The specific processes and techniques used to finish your boxes will depend on how you want to decorate them. You could use cane slices, mokumé gané, imitative materials such as faux ivory or stone, surface texturing, transfers, colored pencils, stencils, paint—whatever you like. (See Chapter 4, *Surface Techniques*.) The choice is yours. Clay veneers were used here.

For added strength and a clean finish, the box decoration is done in two baking stages: lid top and base body, then lid body and base bottom. First, make a sheet of veneer, and decorate it. Cover the top of the lid and the body of the base with the veneer, and bake, open ends up.

When the lid and base have cooled, finish your decoration by covering the body of the lid and the bottom of the base. Note that the wrap covering the lid body conceals the exposed edges of both the structural and decorative tops of the lid, and the base bottom covers the concentric wraps of the bottom's body.

Finally, stand the fully veneered lid and base on your baking tray with open ends up and bake. Once they've cooled, you can finish your decoration with any additional finishing techniques (see page 18).

Variations

Different diameter tubes, and even different shaped forms, can be used to create all sorts of containers with snug lids. For example, I have used smaller wood dowels and metal tubes to make wearable vessels—hollow pendants with space to hold a lucky charm, inspiring message, mad money, or aspirin.

Everlasting Leaves Centerpiece

Artist: Leigh S. Ross

This project uses polymer clay to preserve the natural beauty of Mother Nature's treasures— it's as easy as impressing fresh leaves and flower petals into the clay. The secret to creating flexible, paper-thin leaves and flowers is to mix Sculpey Super Flex with Premo. Sculpey Super Flex tends to be sticky, which can interfere with the impression process. Mixing it with Premo, and leaching if necessary, will reduce this tendency, making the clay easier to roll and handle. Rolling the clay paper-thin may take some practice. Try cooling it off between rollings by laying it in the refrigerator for five minutes, or holding it in front of an air conditioning vent.

Materials

- basic polymer clay equipment and supplies (see page 10)
- white clay (conditioned and leached), Sculpey Super Flex
- clay in leafy and floral colors, Premo
- freshly picked flowers and leaves
- Pearl Ex pigment powder
- 22-gauge craft wire
- spray varnish, such as Krylon Triple-Thick Crystal Clear Glaze Spray
- floral tape
- straw wreath
- E6000 glue
- Kemper Pro Needle Tool
- round tapered Clay Shaper
- pliers
- floral stem wire
- pasta machine
- wire cutters
- glass candle chimney and pillar candle

Getting Started

To prepare leaves, first clean them with dish detergent and water, then lay them on a paper towel to dry. Store them in a phone book to keep them flat until you're ready to use them. To prepare flowers, carefully separate the petals, then keep them in water until you're ready to use them. Lay them on a paper towel, and blot gently to dry them before decorating them with pigment powder.

1 Decorate and position leaves and flowers on the clay sheet.

To make leaves and flowers, mix equal parts of Sculpey Super Flex and the desired color of Premo clay. Roll out the mixture as thin as you can without it sticking, then leach it (See *Leaching* on page 13). Lay the clay sheet on a piece of waxed paper, parchment paper, or office paper.

Apply a layer of Pearl Ex to the underside of the leaves or petals. Spring green, pearl white, and brilliant gold were used here. Gently shake off the excess Pearl Ex and turn the leaves or petals over, placing the powdered sides down on the piece of clay. Press them down gently with your fingertips, but try not to move them around. Do this with as many leaves or petals as you can fit on the sheet of clay, or as many of that variety as you want. It takes 15 to 25 carnation petals to make one flower.

To make leafy accents to cover the base of the flowers, cut a small sheet of the leaf-colored clay, roll it as thin as you can, then apply a layer of green Pearl Ex. Set aside this sheet for baking.

TIP

To make a frilly carnation, the clay should be as thin as possible. Also, leach the clay sheet until it doesn't feel sticky anymore.

2 Impress and cut out the clay leaves and flower petals.

Lay piece of waxed paper over the leaves and petals, again being careful not to move them. Carefully holding the waxed paper in place, roll over the leaves with a brayer, using enough pressure to transfer the texture onto the clay. When this is done correctly, the clay picks up an incredible amount of detail from the leaves and flowers. Gently remove the waxed paper. Using an extra-fine needle tool or a fine needle in a pin vise (the thinner the needle, the easier it cuts the clay), trace around the outline of the leaf, cutting through the clay. Remove the excess clay.

Grab the stem, or the edge of the leaf, and pull it back from the clay. After removing all the real leaves, use the fine needle to clean up the edges of the clay leaves. Gently peel the clay leaves from the waxed paper, and turn them over on the paper, Pearl Ex side down.

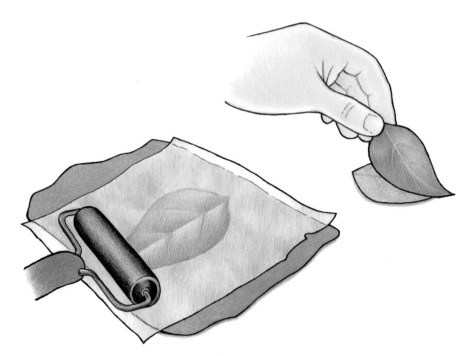

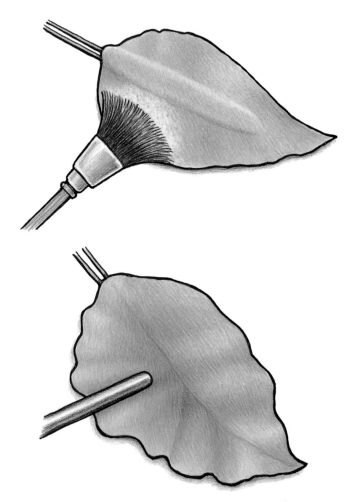

3 Shape and make stems for the clay leaves.

Cut 6" to 10" (15 cm to 25 cm) lengths of 22-gauge craft wire, and fold them tightly in half, with the ends meeting (the size will depend on how long the spine of the leaf is and how much of the leaf you want to have wired). These will be the stems of the leaves.

Lay a folded craft wire on the back of a clay leaf with the fold of the wire about three-quarters of the way up the leaf. Cover the wire with a strip of clay, and trim the excess off at the base of the leaf. Using the back end the Kemper Pro Needle Tool, a clay shaper, or some rounded tool, smooth the edges of the strip into the clay of the leaf. Don't press too hard or you'll smooth out the texture on the other side of the leaf. Then hold the leaf by the wire and cover the back with Pearl Ex.

Depending on the kind of leaf you're using, you'll want to give it a three-dimensional look before it's baked. You can use a rounded tool to carefully stretch the edges a little, which automatically gives you a curly effect on the leaves. You can also use a needle tool to deepen the leaf impressions. Fold the leaf gently along the vein lines that you want to show the most. When you have the look to the leaf that you want, place it down on a piece of paper on your baking pan. Bake at 265° F (129° C) for 40 minutes. Let cool, then seal with a spray varnish that is compatible with polymer clay, such as Krylon Triple-Thick Crystal Clear Glaze Spray.

4 Shape and make the clay flowers.

Shape petals as directed for the leaves, but use a smaller tool such as a round tapered clay shaper. Then, along with the green clay sheet that will be used to cover the base of the flowers, bake at 265° F (129° C) for 40 minutes. Let cool, then seal with spray varnish, such as Krylon Triple-Thick Crystal Clear Glaze Spray.

To make the wire stems, first cut 6" to 10" (15 cm to 25 cm) lengths of 22-gauge craft wire. Use pliers to bend down about 1" (3 cm) of the stem wire, making an elongated loop on one end of the wire; this helps to give you a better base on which to lay the petals while you're assembling the flower. Next, cut about a 2' (61 cm) length of floral tape. Wrap it around the loop of the wire, stretching the tape carefully, yet not too hard. Keep twisting the wire while you hold the tape taut, and run the tape down the wire about three-quarters of the way down.

Now attach the floral tape to the top of the wire again. Grab a couple of petals, preferably petals with tight curly edges. I like to put the tighter curls in the middle and the looser curls on the outside of the flower. Put the base of the petal up against the elongated loop at the top of the wire. Wrap the floral tape over the base of the petal, pulling the tape slightly. Slip in another petal, and wrap the floral tape around the wire a couple times. Add three or four more petals, then twist the tape halfway down the wire, and

break it off. Then start at the top again, attaching the tape to the wire, and add more petals. Keep adding petals evenly around the flower. When your flower is the size you want it, run the floral tape all the way down the wire, and break it off.

Cut a piece from the green clay with scissors. Cut one edge in a zigzag pattern for a decorative finish. Wrap the piece around the base of the flower, and trim off any excess. Using floral tape, secure it to the flower.

5 Assemble the wreath.

Plan the arrangement of the wreath. Position the focal flowers or leaves first. Then, remove them one at a time, coat the bottom of the stems with E6000 glue, and replace them in the same hole. Fill in the rest of the space by using a needle tool to make a hole in the wreath and then inserting a glue-coated wire into the hole. If you're using a straw wreath to assemble your centerpiece, the wires don't need to be any more than 1" (3 cm) long. Continue until all the leaves and flowers are glued in place. Trim the wires as necessary.

Set the pillar candle in the center, and voila! Enjoy your centerpiece. If you plan to burn the candle, place it in a glass sleeve or chimney so the wreath can't catch fire.

Variations

The technique described here is perfect for creating realistic whole flowers; simply wrap the entire stem and add a few wired leaves. Whole flowers, or individual leaves, can be used to make and decorate so many things—try using them to fill a vase, make a wall wreath, decorate a curtain swag, or create custom jewelry. Or build simple polymer clay circles, then attach smaller leaves and flowers to make napkin rings that coordinate with your centerpiece.

Enhancing the Surface

You have luscious-colored clay to work with; you can make intriguing, useful, sturdy structures. So what goes on top? How can you frost this cake?

In about a million ways.

The range of possibilities for surface decoration is one of the most delightful attributes of polymer clay. It works with a host of other art, craft, and commercial materials. You can stamp it, mold it, paint it, emboss it, carve it, antique it, gild it, and transfer words and pictures onto it. It can be used to create anything from a cameolike pendant to an enameled wind chime to a Roman-style mosaic. This easy adaptability inspires artistic experimentation that's bound to lead to exciting discoveries.

Other arts become a banquet of inspiration for polymer clay crafters hungry to play with the clay's surface and create special effects. Paper arts such as rubber stamping, print-making, and bookbinding contribute pigments, paints, inks, glues, colored pencils, irides-cent powders and metallic leaf, photocopies, glitters, and embossing powder. Jewelry contributes carving, inlaying, enameling, texturing, mosaic making, molding, and an-tiquing. Even the kitchen can be raided for cookie cutters, candy molds, and sugarcraft tools for making fancy cake icing.

The interplay between texture, dimension, and surface decoration is another in-triguing aspect of polymer clay crafting. Keep in mind how these elements will interact when planning a project. Because clay can be easily molded, manipulated by hand, or textured with various materials ranging from sandpaper to leaves, there are unlimited combinations to explore.

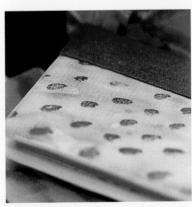

Molded Pine Pendant

Simple elements can be combined to produce elegant work. These pendants have the rich look of antique lacquerware from Japan. You'll make a simple but precise push mold and use it to cast a delicate pine sprig. By building this many-layered piece in stages and baking each one just enough to harden it, you'll keep the all-important surface layer perfect—no need to sand and polish it at the end.

Artist: Jacqueline Lee

Materials

- basic polymer clay equipment and supplies (see page 10)
- 1 yard (.9 m) of black pendant cord
- 2 ounces (57 grams) of Elasticlay
- 1 tiny pinecone
- 1 pine or yew frond
- cardstock
- 1 block of metallic copper clay, Premo
- gold bronzing powder or Pearl Ex powder
- Transparent Liquid Sculpey (TLS)
- 1 block of black clay, either Fimo or Premo

- 2 gold eye pins ½" (1 cm) long
- flat black acrylic paint
- 10" (25 cm) length of black crochet thread, cut in half
- 1 black hairpipe bead 1¼" (3 cm) long
- 1 round black accent bead
- 1 small black bead for necklace closure (hole should be just large enough accommodate a double thickness of the pendant cord)
- toothpick
- pasta machine
- dust mask

- tracing paper
- graph paper
- 2 small pairs of pliers
- small brush

Getting Started

Coat 1" (3 cm) of each end of the pendant cord with cyanoacrylate glue (unless you're using leather), and hang to dry.

1 Make the molds.

Lightly condition the Elasticlay. Shape a small amount into a rectangle that's longer and thicker than your pinecone, and place it on a piece of cardstock. Coat the top of the rectangle with cornstarch, and press down on it lightly with the tile to flatten the surface. Center the pinecone on the clay rectangle, and press gently until it's half submerged. Carefully lift the pinecone straight up out of the clay, which will be your pinecone mold.

Roll some Elasticlay through the pasta machine on setting #1. Place the clay on a piece of cardstock. Gently press the pine frond into the surface of the clay to create an impression.

TIP

You may find it helpful to press the pine needles down with a small piece of clear glass borrowed from a frame. Carefully lift the frond away. Bake both molds according to manufacturer's instructions, and cool completely.

2 Mold and gild the pine parts.

Make a small ball from metallic copper clay. Fill the pinecone mold half full of water, and then press the ball of clay firmly into the mold. (The water will act as a release agent and keep the clay from sticking to the mold.) Expect some water to spill over the sides. Use the tissue blade to trim the clay until it's flush with the mold. It works best to trim from the center toward one end and then turn the mold and repeat. Press a small lump of excess clay gently against the edges of the clay in the mold, and pull back. The lump of clay will stick slightly to the clay in the mold and allow you to pull it out. You may have to repeat the press-and-pull maneuver around the whole outside edge. Repeat to make two molded clay pinecones.

Now you're ready to gild the pinecones. Wearing a dust mask, get a small amount of gold-colored bronzing or Pearl Ex powder on your finger by rubbing your finger around on the inside of the lid. Rub your finger gently over the mold-contoured surface (not the back) of the clay until the raised areas are nicely coated. Bake the pinecones at 275° F (135° C) for 10 minutes.

Roll a sheet of copper clay through the pasta machine on setting #3. Wet the pine frond sheet mold well, and lay the #3 layer of clay on top of it. Run them through the pasta machine together on setting #1. Lay the sheet with the molded copper pine frond on the ceramic tile. Use a sharp craft knife to trim away the excess clay. (Although this step isn't difficult, it does require patience.)

3 Make the pendant body and add the pine parts.

Roll a sheet of copper clay through the pasta machine on setting #1. Lay sandpaper on the clay, grit side down, and run it through the pasta machine on setting #1 again. Gently lift the sandpaper off the clay. The textured surface will be the top layer of your pendant. Lay the clay, textured side up, on a piece of tracing paper, and trim to about 3" (8 cm) square. Place the tracing paper with the textured clay over a piece of graph paper, and use the grid lines to cut out a rectangle of clay large enough to accommodate the pine frond. Round off the corners with your craft knife if desired.

Slowly and carefully lift the pine frond from the tile by running the tissue blade beneath it with (not against) the direction of the needle growth,

as if you're shaving the surface of the tile. Lift the freed end gently with your other hand so that it doesn't adhere back down. When the pine frond is free, lay it on the textured rectangle and gently smooth your finger over it to ensure that all the individual needles are in contact with the clay. Gild the pine frond following step 2.

After the baked pinecones have cooled, turn them over and make scratch marks in several directions on the backs to help them adhere to the next layer. Coat the backs lightly with white glue or TLS, staying away from the edges. Press the baked pinecones onto the pine piece. If this distorts the rectangle, simply place it back over the graph paper, and trim it back into shape. Bake at 275° F (135° C) for 10 minutes.

4 Finish the pendant.

Roll a sheet of black clay at the thickest setting, and place it on a piece of cardstock. This is the back layer. Trim one edge of the clay with a tissue blade; this will be the top edge. Holding an eye pin by the eye with a small pair of pliers, use a second pair of pliers to bend the pin section at a sharp angle. Repeat with the second eye pin. Press the eye pins into the trimmed side of the final layer with the eyes placed ½" to ¾" (1 cm to 2 cm) apart, protruding beyond the edge. Score the back of pine assemblage with a needle tool or craft knife, then press it firmly onto the back layer so that the eye pins are centered at the top and about 1/16" (1.5 mm) of the bottom layer is visible as a border. Trim the edge of the bottom layer all around to leave a 1/16" (1.5 mm) border. Bake at 275° F (135° C) for 20 minutes.

When the pendant has cooled, antique it by applying flat black acrylic paint with a small brush between the pine needles and in the crevices of the pinecone.

5 Assemble the necklace.

Fold a 5" (13 cm) length of black crochet thread in half, and—holding the ends together—thread them through one eye from the side, and draw the thread through until you're left with a dime-size loop of thread on the outside and two long ends in the middle. Lay the pendant face down, and separate the threads. Lay one thread up (perpendicular to the top edge of the pendant) and the other down (perpendicular to the bottom edge). Take care not to pull your loop through the eye.

Place one end of the hairpipe bead into the loop, and lay the bead, centered, across the top edge of the pendant. Grasp the ends of the thread (one in each hand), and pull the loop snugly against the bead. Then tie the thread into a knot against the back of the bead to hold it tightly in place. (You may want to make a double knot to be safe.) Put a tiny dot of cyano-acrylate glue on the knot to secure it. When it's dry, trim away the excess thread. Repeat this process for the other side.

Fold the necklace cord in half. Holding it at the loop end, thread it loop-first (going in at the front out at the back) between the eye pins, beneath the hairpipe bead, until you have a 1½" (4 cm) loop at the back. Fold the loop up, and thread both cord ends through it. Pull snug to form a lark's-head knot around the bead.

Clip the dry, stiffened ends of the pendant cord at an angle with clippers or sharp scissors. Thread both pieces of the pendant cord through an accent bead (it may be easier to do one at a time), and slide the bead into place just above the lark's-head knot.

Thread one end of the pendant cord through the closure bead, then thread the other end through the bead in the opposite direction. The cord should fit snugly in the bead so that when the ends of the cord are pulled to adjust the length it will be held securely in place.

Tie a knot in each cord end. Place a tiny dot of cyanoacrylate glue on the knot to secure it. When the glue is dry, trim the excess.

Variations

This necklace is constructed much like the main project, but instead of using a mold for the design, it's made using two Asian-themed rubber stamps. The main design is the Kanji character for Happiness.

For the top layer—layer one—roll a sheet of black clay through the pasta machine on setting #4. Place the sheet of clay on a piece of tracing paper. Rub gold-colored bronzing powder over just the top surface of the Kanji stamp with your finger, and then stamp an impression into the clay. Trim the clay neatly around the image and bake at 275° F (135° C) for 10 minutes.

For layer two, roll a sheet of black clay through the pasta machine on setting #5, then lay it on a piece of cardstock. Coat the surface of the oriental text stamp with gold powder as before, and press it onto the sheet of clay. When the baked Kanji piece has cooled, score the back, coat it lightly with white glue or TLS, and lay it over the middle layer. Lay a skewer gently against each side of the Kanji layer and use it as a guide to trim a narrow border from the unbaked layer. Bake at 275° F (135° C) for 10 minutes.

For layer three, roll out a small sheet of metallic copper clay on setting #3, then trim it to about a 2" (5 cm) square. Lay it on a corner of a sheet of gold leaf or composite leaf, and trim off excess leaf sheet with a sharp blade. Run the leafed clay through the pasta machine on setting #3 to ensure the leaf adheres well. Run it through again on setting #4. The gold leaf will show tiny cracks. Rotate the leafed clay a quarter turn, and run it through again on setting #5.

When the baked Kanji layers (layers one and two) have cooled, turn the baked piece over, repeat the scoring and gluing process as before, and press the piece firmly onto the leafed layer. Trim the left and right sides of layer three flush with layer two. For the top and bottom borders, lay the bamboo skewer gently against layer two as a guide, but trim the leafed layer about 1/16" (1.5 mm) wider than the skewer. Bake at 275° F (135° C) for 10 minutes.

Make the fourth and final layer following step 4 from the Molded Pine Pendant (you won't need to do any antiquing), and assemble the necklace following step 5.

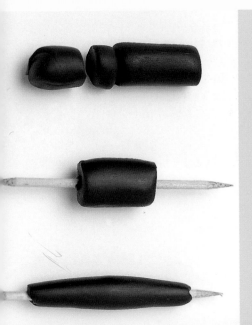

TIP: MAKE A FAUX HAIRPIPE BEAD

Roll a clay snake about the diameter of a pencil, and use a tissue blade to cut a segment about ¾" (2 cm) long. Pierce it lengthwise with a toothpick that has been dusted with cornstarch. Lay the pierced segment on a flat surface. Use two fingers to roll the bead and gradually spread your fingers apart. Roll until the bead lengthens to ¼" (6 mm) from each toothpick end. To bake, suspend the bead above the surface by resting each end of the toothpick on a small piece of excess clay. Bake at 275° F (135° C) for 20 minutes. Trim the bead to size while it's still warm. When it's cool enough to handle, hold the bead in one hand, and use pliers to pull out the toothpick; it may help to twist the toothpick first and then pull. Use the tissue blade to trim off the rough ends of the bead so that it's about the same width as the pendant.

Mosaic Plaque

Artist: Margaret R

Creating a polymer clay mosaic can be thrilling, because there's no limit to the colors that can be used, as there is with other mosaic materials. The "water" in this mosaic was created by blending blue and translucent clay with embossing powder in various amounts to create an array of shades. The final result is a beautiful water scene with shimmery depth and sophistication. This ungrouted mosaic was created by placing uncured "tiles" on an uncured background, eliminating the need for adhesive. The resulting classic look is reminiscent of the intricate, expressive works created by the ancient Romans.

Materials

- basic polymer clay equipment and supplies (see page 10)
- picture for reference and tracing
- 1 block of white clay, Fimo or Premo
- 1 block of translucent clay, Fimo or Premo
- dark blue embossing powder
- 1 block of blue clay, Fimo or Premo
- 1 block of black clay, Fimo or Premo
- 1 block of yellow clay, Fimo or Premo
- imitation gold leaf
- tracing paper
- matte varnish, Fimo or Sculpey
- pasta machine
- tapestry needle
- penny or penny-size circular cutter
- paint brush

Getting Started

Be sure to include the most important details when tracing an image for a mosaic, such as the eye, fins, and gills of this fish.

1 Transfer the mosaic pattern to the clay.

First, trace the selected image in pencil. Next, use a pasta machine to roll out a piece of clay about 3½" x 2¾" (9 cm x 7 cm) on setting #1. Make the rectangle as even as possible, but don't trim the edges. Place the clay on a bakeable work surface.

Then lay the tracing face up on the rectangle of clay, and smooth it out. Run a tapestry needle over the lines of the pattern to create slight but visible indentations in the clay. Remove the paper after tracing all the lines.

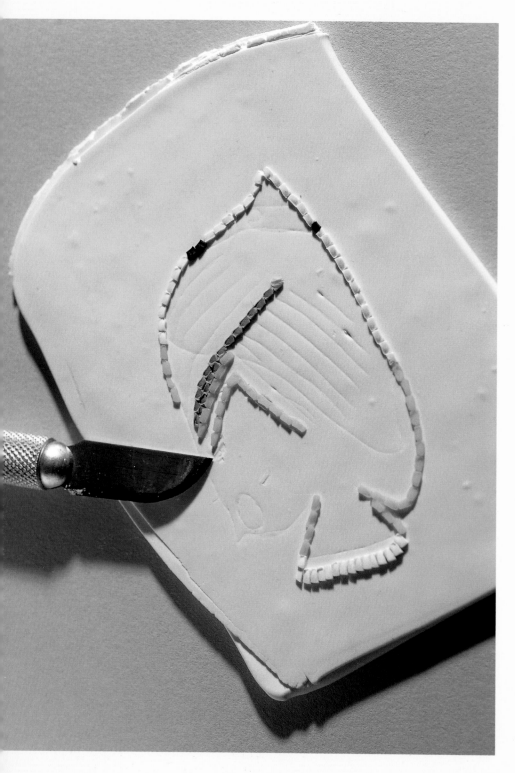

2 Fill in the traced pattern with tiles.

Roll out the clay to be used for the tiles on setting #5, and place the slabs on baking parchment or waxed paper. From these slabs, cut several short strips ⅛" to ³⁄₁₆" (3 mm to 4 mm) wide. Using a craft knife with a curved or angled blade, cut small squares from the strips, and begin placing the tiles along the image outline.

To create the shades of blue for the water, first roll out a sheet of translucent clay using a pasta machine on setting #1 (the thickest setting). Then, cut out a 1½" x 1½" (4 cm x 4 cm) from this sheet. Mix in about ¼ to ½ teaspoon of embossing powder, a little bit at a time, until the clay is denim blue. Cut the clay into four equal pieces. Set one aside to be used as is. Then cut out six penny-size pieces of clay from the remainder of the translucent sheet, using a craft knife and a penny or a circle cutter as a guide. Mix one piece of translucent clay with one denim blue piece; two pieces of translucent clay with another denim blue piece; and the remaining three translucent pieces with the last denim blue piece. Finally, create a blue-gray color by mixing 2 parts white, ½ part blue, ½ part black clay. For the gold accent tiles, roll translucent clay through the pasta machine on setting #6 (very thin). Then, carefully lay the metal leaf on top and smooth it out.

TIP

To make an eye like the one seen here, press a small ball of clay into place with a ball stylus tool or ball-headed pin.

TIP

To enable you to hang the plaque, adhere a looped string to the back using permanent glue, or drill two holes at the top for a knotted cord. A smaller piece would make a striking brooch or pendant.

3 Fill in the remaining parts of the image.

For guidance and inspiration, refer to the image used to create the traced pattern. Fill in the major features, such as the fish's stripes and spots, then continue with the background. Place the tiles in rows to keep the mosaic neat. Pay attention to the flow of the lines that the rows create. The tiles in the body of the fish here have been laid in diagonal rows, but the tail is made up of horizontal rows; this helps to define the image

and creates movement in the piece. To create the illusion of water, alternate between shades of blue, and lay the tiles in wavy lines as seen here.

Once the mosaic is complete, put a piece of blank tracing paper over the tiles and use a smooth roller, such as a brayer or jar, to gently embed them into the slab of clay. Then remove the tracing paper, and bake according to the manufacturer's directions. Once the piece is cool, finish with two coats of matte varnish.

Variations

Like all surface techniques, this one could be used to ornament many different objects. Glue your plaque to a plain journal cover, clock case, or vase. Want to wear it as a brooch? Add a pinback (first clean the metal with alcohol, roughen it with a nail file, then glue it to the plaque with cyanoacrylate glue). Make a mosaic disk to fit commercial bezels for a pendant, earrings, ring, or brooch.

I work wet-on-wet, but that isn't the only way to make polymer clay mosaics. Some artists place prebaked "tiles" ranging from tiny threads to substantial pieces on top of unbaked clay. And some artists make canes that look like mosaics.

Wind Play Wind Chime

Artist: Linda Goff

*Make this unique wind chime using polymer clay and color-plated aluminum tooling foil. The basic form is easily made using an ordinary jar as a support. Transparent Liquid Sculpey mixed with powdered pigments was used to glaze and reinforce the delicate embossed foil elements. The clay elements were carved using a **V**-shaped linoleum cutting tool; try using wood-carving tools of various shapes as well. Be sure to hang the finished wind chime where it will receive some protection from the sun and weather, such as a window or a porch.*

Materials

- basic polymer clay equipment and supplies (see page 10)
- 4 conditioned blocks of gold polymer clay
- chime tubes
- 2 conditioned blocks of polymer clay in assorted colors
- cotton swabs
- tracing paper
- tooling foil
- Transparent Liquid Sculpey (TLS)
- Sculpey Diluent
- metallic pigment powders

- acrylic and oil paints
- E-6000 glue or other two-part adhesive
- water-based satin varnish, such as Flecto Varathane Diamond Elite (black and silver can)
- nylon or heavy cotton thread
- 20-gauge wire
- metal ring for hanging the chime
- pasta machine
- cylindrical glass jar about 13" (33 cm) in circumference
- rubber stamp
- linoleum cutter with **V**-shaped blade

- bone folder
- stylus tools for embossing the foil
- stack of newspapers at least ¼" (6 mm) thick
- scissors
- paint palette
- round-nosed jewelry pliers

Getting Started

Design shapes for the foil accents that will be applied to the body of the wind chime by sketching ideas on tracing paper. Then cut them out to make flexible templates that can be easily used on a curved surface.

1 Make the body of the wind chime.

Roll the gold clay through the pasta machine on the thickest setting. Trim that clay so the sheet is 3" x 14" (8 cm x 36 cm). Cut away the top edge to create a decorative pattern and the bottom edge to create a wave pattern. Wrap the clay sheet around a cylindrical glass jar so the short ends overlap, and make sure they're aligned. Press a rubber stamp into the overlapped clay so it stays on the jar. Bake following the manufacturer's directions. Don't remove the clay from the jar.

2 Carve the body of the wind chime.

With a pencil, trace the templates of the foil accents on the body of the wind chime. Then carve decorative lines around the shapes and other areas of the body using a linoleum cutter. Fill the carved lines with conditioned clay in a contrasting color. Remove any excess clay using a bone folder, cotton swabs, and isopropyl alcohol. Bake following the manufacturer's directions. Once the clay has cooled, carve more decorative lines between the filled lines. Leave the new lines unfilled.

3 Make foil shapes.

Using a pencil, trace the same templates used on the body of the wind chime on the front of the tooling foil. The traced outlines should be slightly larger than the templates. Next, place the foil on a stack of newspapers at least ¼" (6 mm) thick, then emboss and/or pierce the foil with a stylus tool, paper punch, or needle tool. Embossing the front (here, the green side) of the foil will create a re-cessed pattern; embossing the back (here, the silver side), a raised pattern. After embossing, neatly trim the foil to the edges using scissors.

4 Decorate the body of the wind chime.

Fill three sections of a paint palette halfway with TLS. Thin with TLS diluent according to manufacturer's directions. Tint the TLS by mixing a small amount of metallic pigment powder into it. (More powder will yield a more opaque color and less powder a lighter, more translucent color.) Brush a layer of colored TLS onto the embossed foil shapes, and let it settle into the recessed areas. The brush can be cleaned with turpentine, paint thinner, or isopropyl alcohol. Bake the foil, TLS side facing up, for 20 minutes follow-ing the manufacturer's directions. Once they've cooled, decorate them with acrylic paint. Then use E-6000 glue or similar two-part adhesive to attach the foil accents to the body of the wind chime—but make sure you follow the glue manufacturer's directions exactly. Apply a fairly thick layer of glue on both the foil piece and the body, wait about 10 minutes, then press them firmly together. Remove the body of the wind chime from the jar.

TIP

Once the foil is coated with TLS, the colored surface can be easily wiped away, before curing, to reveal the silver metal underneath. Try wiping only the raised areas of the accents to make them stand out. Use a dry paper towel wrapped around a finger to remove the color.

5 Make and attach dangles to the body of the wind chime.

Roll some clay through the pasta machine on the third thickest setting. Cut shapes from the sheet of clay, and bake them on a flat or curved surface, such as a jar, for 30 minutes. Once the dangles have cooled, decorate both sides using the same techniques described in steps 2, 3, and 4 for decorating the body of the wind chime. Also make some dangles entirely of foil. Apply water-based satin varnish, such as Flecto Varathane Diamond Elite, to all areas of baked TLS to prevent scratches. Then drill a hole about ¼" (6 mm) from the top edge of each dangle. Also drill a hole for each dangle or row of dangles on the bottom edge of the body of the wind chime. Next, attach the dangles at various lengths using nylon or heavy cotton thread.

6 Attach the chime tubes.

Measure the diameter of the wind chime body, and cut a length of 20-gauge wire twice as long. Using round-nosed jewelry pliers, bend V shapes in the wire to hold each chime tube in place. The tubes should be positioned far enough apart to hang separately when still, but close enough together so they chime when moved gently. Drill two holes in the top of the body directly opposite from each other. Thread the ends of the wire through the holes and bend the ends to secure. Clip off any excess wire. Next, hang the chime tubes from the wire using nylon or heavy cotton thread. Make a wind catcher by hanging one of your large foil dangles through the inside of a chime tube so it is about 2" (5 cm) below the bottom of the tube. To hang the wind chime, first drill four equally spaced holes in the body of the wind chime, about ¼" (6 mm) from the top edge. Then, thread a piece of nylon through two of the holes, directly opposite each other, and tie securely. Repeat the procedure with the other two holes to create an **X**. Finally, cut another piece of nylon, and tie one end to a large metal ring; tie the other end around the center of the **X**.

Variations

Try using the construction technique described here to build a mobile, such as a suncatcher. Use translucent clay for the dangles, then carve and backfill to create an opaque pattern. When sunlight hits the clay, the interplay between dark and light will be charming. Experiment with dangles of varying thickness, different shapes and sizes of carving tools, and clay inclusions such as glitter. Be sure to sand and buff the baked clay for the most translucent effect.

Book Covers with Freehand Transfers

Artist: Meredith Arnold

This freehand design, drawn with artist's felt-tipped pens on a scrap of synthetic fabric, was transferred to raw polymer clay using ordinary isopropyl alcohol. The result is a controlled yet flowing design, reminiscent of watercolors. For durable book covers, use a strong polymer clay that has some flexibility after it's baked, such as Fimo or Premo. Sculpey III isn't suitable. It's also a good idea to experiment with this technique first before finalizing the design of the book covers. Try combining different colors, simple and detailed designs, and various amounts of alcohol.

Materials

- basic polymer clay equipment and supplies (see page 10)
- 2 pieces of cardstock, 2" x 5 ½" (5 cm x 14 cm), folded lengthwise
- 2 paper clamps, 1" (3 cm) size
- precut stack of paper, 2" x 2 ¾" x ½" (5 cm x 7 cm x 1 cm) deep or less
- tight-weave cheesecloth or machine-made lace, 2" x 2" (5 cm x 5 cm)
- 1 piece of kraft paper or lightweight brown paper bag, 2" x 2" (5 cm x 5 cm)
- 1 block of white or light-colored clay
- Berol Prismacolor felt-tipped pens
- polyvinyl acetate (PVA) glue, such as Crafter's Pick Ultimate Glue
- masking tape
- thin synthetic fabric, such as coat lining material, 6" x 7" (15 cm x 18 cm)
- unlined index cards
- cotton swabs
- leather or Ultrasuede for binding
- bone folder or spoon
- small paint brush
- scissors
- pasta machine (optional)

Getting Started

Many copy centers offer paper-cutting services and charge by the number of cuts, regardless of paper quantity. This project uses a stack of 8 ½" x 11" (22 cm x 28 cm) paper cut into four equally sized smaller stacks.

1 Make the book block.

Crease the folds of the cardstock sharply, using a bone folder or the back of a spoon. Place the folded cardstock pieces on either side of the stack of paper, in the same orientation. (The folded edges should align with what will be the spine of the book.) Next, make sure the pages and cardstock are squared up, then attach paper clamps to both bottom corners of the paper block as shown. This will allow the block to stand freely on the work surface.

Fan the pages of the paper block in one direction, then apply a light coat of white PVA glue to the spine with a small paintbrush. Fan the pages in the opposite direction and apply another light coat of PVA glue. Squeeze the pages of the block together tightly, then lay the cheesecloth over the spine. Pull on the longer edges of the cheesecloth to hold the pages together tightly until the glue squishes through the weave. Hold in position for about 1 minute to allow the glue to set.

Once the pages remain together tightly without being held, apply another light coat of glue on top of the cheesecloth, and place the kraft paper over it. Burnish along the spine, and wipe off any excess glue. You now have a book block. Place the block between two sheets of waxed paper, and weigh it down for about 10 minutes. Once the glue has set, remove the waxed paper. Trim the kraft paper and cheesecloth to no less than ¼" (6 mm) from the spine, on all sides.

Make a template for the book cover by tracing the book block on a piece of cardstock. Make the rectangle ½" (1 cm) longer and wider then cut it out.

2 Make and decorate the book cover.

Roll out a 5" x 6" (13 cm x 15 cm) sheet of polymer clay using a pasta machine on a medium setting, such as #4. Place the sheet on a piece of paper, and set aside.

Tape a piece of waxed paper to the work surface. Tape the edges of the synthetic fabric to the waxed paper, making sure the fabric is taut. Using Berol Prismacolor felt-tipped pens, decorate the fabric. The ink will bleed, so choose colors that will blend well, and leave some open space in the design to compensate.

Next, place the decorated fabric on the polymer clay sheet, ink side down. Put an index card over the fabric, and burnish with a bone folder or the back of a spoon. Make sure the fabric completely adheres to the clay surface. Then, dampen a cotton swab with isopropyl alcohol; squeeze out the excess. Gently dab the fabric with the cotton swab, making sure the fabric stays adhered to the clay. Some of the pigment will appear on the cotton swab; this indicates that the transfer process is working. If the fabric becomes so saturated that it buckles, stop applying the isopropyl alcohol and just burnish it back in place; the end result will be different from the intended design, but still attractive. More moisture intensifies the watercolor effect, but if too much is used, it will ruin the transfer. Place an index card over the fabric and burnish to blot up excess liquid and pigment. Allow the fabric to dry for 3 minutes, then remove the index card.

Using the book cover template, carefully cut out two pieces of the decorated clay. Place the clay on an index card on a baking sheet. Bake at 265° F (129° C) for 25 minutes. If the clay pieces warp during baking, immediately place index cards over them, and weigh them down while they cool.

Using the rough side of an emery board or extra-fine sanding block, lightly sand the undecorated sides of the clay under running water; this will allow the glue to adhere better. Then, sand the edges of the covers while holding them together to ensure that they end up the same size and shape.

TIP

If a pasta machine isn't available, roll the clay to the thickness of a computer diskette. Place diskettes to the left and right of the clay, and tape in place. Roll over the clay and diskettes with a rolling pin or brayer.

3 Assemble the book.

To avoid accidentally gluing the book shut, place a piece of waxed paper between the glued cover and first page of the book block. Apply glue to the front of the book block, on the cardstock. Carefully position the book block over the undecorated side of one clay book cover. Make sure the spine edges are aligned and the other three sides of the cardstock are centered on the clay book cover. Press down firmly, then wipe off any excess glue with a dampened paper towel. Repeat the procedure to adhere the back cover of the book. Place a weight on the book, and let it dry.

4 Cover the spine.

Cut a rectangular strip of leather slightly larger than 2" x 1¼" (5 cm x 3 cm). Center the leather over the spine to check the fit. It should overlap the book covers; trim if necessary. Spread PVA glue carefully and evenly on the underside of the leather. Then, center it on the spine and press into place, making sure the corners are secure. Wipe off any excess glue, stroking away from the leather. Be careful; it can be difficult to remove glue from leather. Let dry before using.

Variations

Use rubber stamps to make impressions on the unbaked clay covers. After baking, apply acrylic paint with a dampened paper towel. Not all brands of acrylic paint work well on polymer clay; a few that do include Plaid Folk Art, Delta Ceramcoat, and Liquitex paints, available at most U.S. craft-supply outlets. For a slate effect, apply white paint to black clay. Wipe away excess, leaving some paint in the recessed rubber stamp impressions for a patina effect.

Decorate the cover with other types of transfers.

Basic transfers are created from carbon-based toner images. Either photocopied or laser-printed images will work if the toner contains carbon. If the transfer isn't successful when you use the following process, the image doesn't contain the necessary carbon to transfer. Roll out a sheet of clay with a nice flat surface. Burnish image onto the sheet of clay. Apply isopropyl alcohol to the back of the image with a cotton swab. The paper should become translucent-like. Blot any excess rubbing alcohol using an index card or other piece of paper. Let dry for half a minute or so and gently remove. The image should be very dark and crisp.

Laminated Boxes

Artist: Ellen Marshall

This project highlights the compatibility of polymer clay, rubber stamping, and paper arts supplies. The Chinese "take-out" box seen here was made using a simple one-piece paper foundation that was laminated with decorated clay. First the sheets of clay are textured with sandpaper, then they're painted with artist's inks to create vibrantly colored patterns. After the paint is dry, the unbaked clay can be cut apart and arranged in various ways, such as the delightful striped pattern on this "take-out" box. These miniature treasures make cherished party favors. A bigger box could hold a gift of candy or cookies, but make sure the treats are well sealed in plastic wrap.

Materials

- basic polymer clay equipment and supplies (see page 10)
- durable, heavyweight paper such as cardstock
- acrylic paints in assorted colors
- Transparent Liquid Sculpey (TLS)
- ¼ block of clay in a color to match the box, for a 2" (5 cm) box (larger boxes require more clay)
- 2 blocks of clay in a light color
- heat-resistant double-sided mounting tape in ¼" (6 mm) and ¾" (2 cm) rolls (such as Terrifically Tacky Tape)
- decorative paper cord for box handle
- artist's inks in assorted colors
- photocopier
- sponges and rubber stamps
- pigments and ink pads
- pasta machine
- small paintbrushes
- chambered watercolor palette
- soft makeup brush

Getting Started

We built the boxes for this project from scratch, using a commercially available box template. But it isn't necessary to build a box; any paper or cardboard box can be decorated using this technique.

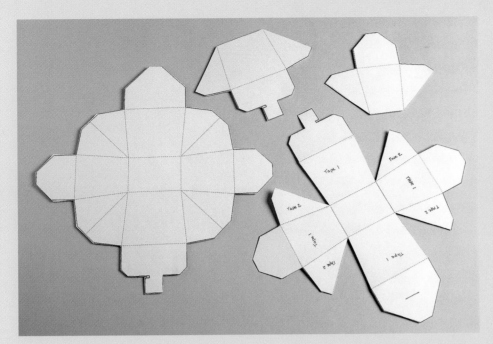

1 Prepare the templates.

Photocopy the template for the paper foundation box (see below) onto a piece of durable, heavyweight paper such as cardstock. Cut along the solid lines of the template with a craft knife. Then, cut along the edges of the two wider sides of the box, and remove the resulting triangles of paper. The narrower sides of the box will now have flaps for folding and securing the box. Lightly score the remaining dotted lines, then fold them in the same direction. Also, cut a slit in the middle of the box top, opposite the closing tab. If desired, make smaller templates of the box sides for use in planning the surface design.

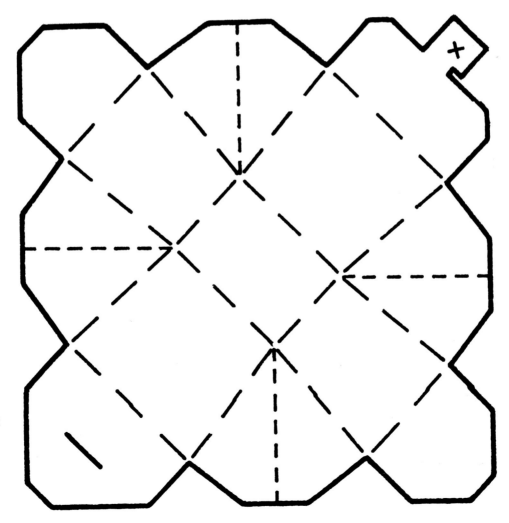

After folding, cut slot in this cover piece for tab **X**

2 Decorate the foundation box and the clay.

Sponge or rubber stamp pigment ink on the entire inside of the box and the fronts of the box's top flaps. Paint the bottom and the folded edges on the outside of the box with acrylic paint; once dry, paint over these areas again with TLS, which will strengthen the paper. Bake following the manufacturer's directions.

Roll out sheets of clay using a pasta machine on a fairly thin setting. Make two 7" x 8" (18 cm x 20 cm) sheets of clay, piecing smaller sheets together to achieve the size, if necessary. (Boxes larger than the one shown here require more clay.) Dust the backs lightly with baby powder, and lay the sheets on pieces of cardboard.

Cover the clay sheets with plastic wrap and then with a piece of sandpaper, and use a roller to press the sandpaper into the clay, to create texture. Then, use a palette knife to loosen the clay sheet from the cardboard. Remove the sandpaper and plastic wrap. Now the clay is ready to decorate. Use brushes, stamps, or sponges to apply inks, let dry, then apply additional ink or painted accents. Use ink sparingly; if applied too heavily, it will collect in the recessed areas of the clay surface. Pearlescent and metallic colors were used on these boxes.

TIP

Inks can be dried more quickly with a hair dryer. Just be sure to use a cool setting.

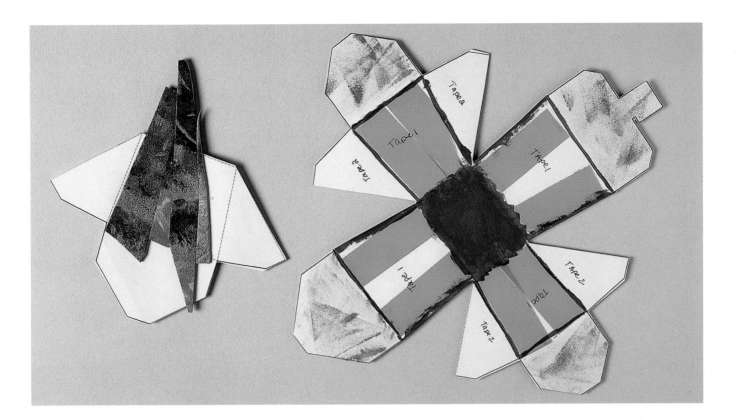

3 Laminate and construct the box.

To plan the laminated design, cut strips of clay using a sharp craft knife and a metal ruler, and arrange them on the smaller templates.

Apply double-sided mounting tape to the template. Use two strips of tape for each panel of the box that will face outward when it's folded together, as seen here. Remove the protective cover strip to reveal the adhesive. Brush TLS over the box panels, making sure that the exposed tape is covered. Then, cut strips of clay and arrange them on each panel. Bake following the clay manufacturer's directions. When the box has cooled, carefully paint the edges of the clay panels with acrylic paint. Let dry.

Next, apply one piece of double-sided mounting tape to each of the four box flaps, close to, but not on, the areas that will be folded. Trim any excess tape. To construct the box, remove the protective cover strip from one flap. Fold the flap and the whole panel toward the inside of the box. Then fold the adjacent panel toward the inside of the box, bringing the edges of both panels together. Make sure they're aligned, then press them firmly together. Repeat with the remaining flaps.

Brush a little TLS into each corner edge of the box. Using the colored clay, roll thin snakes and fill the corner edges, smoothing the clay out so

it's flush with the box. Bake following the manufacturer's directions for the clay, and let cool.

To make the handle, drill holes on opposite sides of the box. Thread the ends of a pretty paper cord from the outside into the holes, then knot the ends of the cord on the inside of the box.

Stand by Celie Fago

Variations

A cohesive mosaic design can be created using unbaked sheets of clay in various colors, all decorated with a single design in coordinating colors. Start with sheets of unbaked clay. Apply the design by stamping, stenciling, or silk screening it, and let the clay dry. Build the mosaic by cutting strips or blocks from the decorated sheets and fitting them together on a thin, unbaked foundation sheet. When you're satisfied with the arrangement, cover the clay with tissue paper, and roll gently over the tissue with a roller to adhere the mosaic pieces to the foundation sheet. Cut the clay as desired to shape it. You can use the sheet flat, draped like fabric, or wrapped around a bead or box; bake following the manufacturer's directions.

Exploring Precious Metal Clay by Celie Fago

Almost Alchemy:
The Story of Precious Metal Clay

When I first heard about Precious Metal Clay (PMC) I thought I had misunderstood. I'd been working with polymer clay, making jewelry for about seven years, and apprenticing to a metalsmith, studying metalworking for seven years. A clay that turned to precious metal when fired? Impossible. A few months later in 1998 a colleague showed me a bead made with this same new material. The bead had a look to it, a deeper texture than you could get with any metals technique I knew, and a resonance with its companion polymer beads that I couldn't quite identify. I was transfixed. The rest, as they say, is history. Like most people I didn't believe it possible—at first. Now, although its story has become as familiar in the telling as my own, I still marvel at the magic of a metal whose history is as a clay; I still marvel at the magic of PMC.

It was only after working with PMC for those first six months in 1998 that I discarded the idea that it was simply a shortcut to metalwork. Like polymer clay, PMC is a pioneer material and a clay. Understanding the nature of a material that's clay then metal has caused me to move away from attempts to replicate silversmithing and toward an understanding that an essential quality of great metal clay jewelry is the vestigial "clayness" found in the best PMC work. An undefinable quality, a range of textural effects that defy its recent history as clay but distinguish it forever from cast or fabricated silver. Whereas PMC is in its infancy, having been invented a mere 7 years ago, polymer clay is in its adolescence. The skills honed in working with polymer clay lend themselves splendidly to PMC. They are excellent companions. The pure silver adds aesthetic richness and, since it's precious metal, actual value to the polymer. Polymer clay, for its part, offers PMC the glory of color.

Precious Metal Clay Basic Techniques

This revolutionary new material was invented by Mitsubishi Materials Corporation of Sanda, Japan. It consists of three ingredients: tiny particles of pure silver (or pure gold), water, and an organic binder. When it's wet, or fresh, it's claylike and malleable and can be sculpted, textured, rolled, pushed into a press mold, or draped around a kernel of cereal to create a hollow form bead. When it's s air dried or leather-hard, it can be carved, cut, filed, drilled, and joined to make complex forms. When PMC is fired in a small electric kiln, the water evaporates, and the binder burns away.

The material shrinks as the metal particles fuse together, sharpening the surface detail, leaving an object made of pure silver. PMC comes in lump form (silver and gold), paste (or slip), and sheet. It also comes prepackaged in a syringe and can be extruded to ornament a surface. Several related products are in development.

This chapter covers the basic techniques for working with PMC. I have also included many tips and techniques that I have discovered and developed while using this unique material. The projects that follow range from simpler beads and earrings to more elaborate frames and pendants. I hope that they provide inspiration and a useful base of techniques on which to build your own designs.

Composition

Precious Metal Clay (PMC) is composed of three ingredients—fine pure silver particles so small they could be described as a flour, a proprietary binder, and water. The binder is organic, naturally occurring and nontoxic. Water accounts for 10 to 20 percent of the material. The silver powder and the binder are stable, but the water content begins to evaporate as soon as the package is opened, or over time, with improper storage.

PMC comes in four different forms: lump (silver and gold), sheet, paste, and packaged in a syringe.

- **Lump**—Silver lump PMC comes in two types: standard PMC and PMC Plus. The former was invented about 7 years ago by Mitsubishi Materials Corporation of Sanda, Japan; it shrinks 28 percent when fired. A few years later, that same company developed a new clay called PMC Plus. Because of a key difference in the silver particles that make up PMC Plus, it's stronger after firing than standard PMC, and it shrinks by only 12 percent.

- **PMC Plus sheet**—The 2" x 2" (60 mm x 60 mm) square sheet is a paper thin, specially formulated material that's had its moisture content stabilized and therefore isn't subject to evaporation. It resembles ultra suede, is flexible like fabric, and doesn't dry out.

- **PMC Plus paste**—This form is prepackaged slip.

- **PMC Plus prepackaged in a syringe**—This is specially formulated slip that doesn't slump when you extrude it onto a surface. It can be used for decoration or for repairs.

Sheet, paste, and syringe style PMC are all formulated from PMC Plus and should be fired accordingly. You can unwrap a package of PMC and use the entire ounce in making a small vessel, or you can stretch an ounce, economically, and make many smaller pieces. The textured leaf shapes shown on page 102, were two of seventy-two such shapes made from 1 ounce of standard PMC.

Keeping PMC Moist

Two discoveries I made early on made working with PMC immeasurably easier. The first has to do with extending the working time of fresh PMC by rolling through plastic wrap to minimize evaporation. The second has to do with working leather-hard. Borrowed from ceramics, the term *leather-hard* simply means "dry" when used to describe PMC. It may mean air dried, or force dried under a light or in an oven set at 225° to 285° F. For all intents and purposes, when the material is dry or leather-hard it's stable indefinitely.

Standard versus Plus

Because of their slightly different balance of ingredients, PMC and PMC Plus have different attributes in all three stages—fresh, leather-hard, and as metal after firing. Fresh standard PMC takes detail beautifully. It rarely requires oil to prevent sticking, and it's both flexible and strong while leather-hard. PMC Plus rebounds slightly from texture, so the impression isn't always as crisp as that of standard. It's slightly more difficult to join to itself, and when fresh, it always requires oil to prevent sticking. PMC Plus has less binder holding the metal particles together so when it's leather-hard it's not as durable as standard. It's fragile and care must be taken not to bump or drop a piece. Besides taking details of impressions a bit better to begin with, standard PMC sharpens detail because it shrinks more, whereas the 12 percent shrinkage of Plus doesn't have much effect on detail. After firing however, it's denser and stronger than fired standard PMC, so PMC Plus is more appropriate for rings and thinner designs. Because it has more binder, standard PMC is remarkably strong in its leather-hard stage, and as a result, it carves more easily than PMC Plus. Leather-hard standard PMC can be successfully cut with a protected tissue blade, but this same method may shatter leather-hard PMC Plus. Instead, use a jeweler's saw with a 3/0 blade for PMC Plus. Both materials can be drilled with a hand drill, a Dremel, or a flex shaft.

Storage

Store PMC tightly wrapped in plastic, in its original package, and in airtight plastic bags with folded-up wet paper towels inside. Refresh the paper towels on a regular basis, especially if you live in a dry climate. If you discover that a package of clay seems dry when you push your finger into it, take a bit of sponge or paper towel, dampen it, and put it in the package under the tightly wrapped PMC.

Rehydrating

To rehydrate rock hard PMC, stab holes in it with a needle tool, then run it under the tap (or use distilled water) for 30 to 60 seconds. Rewrap it tightly in plastic along with a tablespoon or two of water. In several hours it will reabsorb the water and give slightly to the pressure of your finger. Repeat the above process, but instead of running it under water, stab holes in it, then wrap it tightly with some water in with the clay. You may be able to knead the clay at this point, or you may need to repeat the first steps one or two more times. Once you have some experience with PMC, you'll be able to recognize a good working consistency, and remember that you can always turn clay into slip by adding extra water.

Forming

Rolling out PMC: As a general rule, if you flip your PMC over every three or four rolls, it is much less likely to stick to your work surface.

Water versus oil: What to do about cracking PMC?

When closing a joint in fresh PMC, or joining one fresh piece to another—like an embellishment to a bead—you'll need to add a bit of water. After you've made the joint, it's helpful to smooth it over with an oiled finger or oiled brush handle. Experiment, and you'll soon know when you need to switch from water to oil. Too much water will make mud. If this happens, wait a few seconds, then smooth over the wet spot with an oiled finger. Balancing the moisture level simply takes some getting used to. Keep your water and your oil within reach.

Tenting

If your PMC is cracking, roll it out through plastic or try "tenting"—that is, tearing off a large sheet of plastic and working under it. Put a barrier up to protect your work area from any breeze. Or, try rehearsing a particular design in scrap polymer clay until you can work a bit faster.

Top left: PMC Plus; top right: Standard PMC; below: PMC Sheet.

Setup and Tools

Although your PMC will ultimately be transformed into metal, you'll do most of your work in PMC while it's clay. Both philosophically and in the matter of tools, this is an important consideration. Here are a few essential tools. Generally the tools you use for polymer clay will work with PMC.

- For rolling polymer clay, I use a 1½" (4 cm) diameter PVC pipe, available at a hardware store. For PMC, I use a ½" (about 1 cm) diameter PVC pipe **(A),** 6" to 7" (about 15 cm) long (both cut with a tube cutter).

- For cutting fresh PMC, use a tissue blade, a Nu-Blade, or a craft knife **(B)**. On leather-hard standard PMC, use a protected tissue blade. (Glue two Popsicle sticks with 5-minute Epoxy onto either side of the dull edge.) A hard blade may shatter leather-hard PMC Plus. Instead, use a jeweler's saw with a 3/O blade.

- A small airtight container **(C)** is another essential for storing slip. A plastic film canister will do, but small round pill containers with attached tops are even better. They are typically sold in twos, giving you one for PMC Plus and one for standard PMC. PMC Plus is grayish white, whereas stan-

dard PMC is more of a buff or tan color. Remember to label your containers.

- I use and recommend two brushes **(D)**: a small, pointed watercolor brush for applying slip or water and a square-tipped one, kept clean, to remove excess slip.

- Use foam rubber scraps (¼" to ½" [5 mm to 1 cm] thick) from a fabric store **(E),** accordion folded, and stuffed into a cup for drying delicate assemblies. Laid flat on your work surface, foam pieces give you a place to dry rounded PMC objects so they won't develop a flat side.

- Teflon sheet **(F)** is sold as nonstick baking sheets in kitchen stores and as Teflon Pressing Sheets in fabric stores. They can be cut up into convenient palette sizes, or you can roll directly on them. If you don't have access to Teflon, plastic report covers, sold in stationary stores, are another possibility, but I strongly recommend Teflon.

Work surfaces

Many materials can be used as a work surface—for example, glass, marble, Plexiglas, acrylic, a laminated place mat, or a plastic report cover. Any smooth, nonporous surface will do. I use

and recommend only glass—not window glass, which is dangerously thin, but a 10" x 15" (25 cm x 38 cm) sheet of ¼" (6.5 mm) plate glass **(G),** with smoothed edges. It's inexpensive, and it's available from auto glass stores. It makes an excellent surface because PMC doesn't readily stick to it, and it isn't scratched by cutting blades. What's more, a lump of PMC set on the glass and covered with plastic will remain viable for 24 to 48 hours. If you won't be working for more than a day, invert a dish over the plastic on top of the PMC to seal it on the work surface. For a shorter duration, dip your finger in water and run it around the PMC on the work surface, and press the plastic wrap to seal it.

Other tools

- A small container **(H)** with a section of kitchen sponge pushed into it, full of water. You can use a paper cup trimmed to 1" (3 cm) height. Keep the water level high enough so that you can easily get some water on the end of your brush.

- Another small container **(I),** with a piece of foam rubber in it, filled with olive oil. Olive oil is specifically recommended because it's less likely to get sticky and rancid.

- A pin tool **(J)**
- A small spray bottle full of water **(K)**
- Plastic wrap **(L).** I recommend Saran because it's heavy, and it doesn't stretch or cling; avoid waxed paper of any sort.
- Rolling rectangle **(M)**—that is, a 2 ½" x 7" (6 cm x 18 cm) piece of plate glass or rigid plastic to use for rolling ropes of clay or "wire"
- Scrap polymer clay, for rehearsing ideas and for securing a texture to a work surface
- Palette knife **(N)** in plastic or metal for making slip
- Good pair of fine tweezers **(O)**
- Brass tube sections **(P)** are useful for cutting out circles of PMC.
- Use drinking straws **(Q)** for cutting out circles of clay.
- Stacks of playing cards **(R)** help you roll consistent thicknesses of PMC.
- Foam rubber **(S)**, accordion-folded and pushed into a cup, affords a good place for drying delicate PMC assemblies.
- A brass sliding millimeter gauge **(T)**
- Fine sandpaper (320, 400, 600, and 1,000 grit)
- Micron-graded polishing paper (1,200 grit, from a jewelry supplier)
- Salon boards—double sided, medium fine (from a pharmacy)
- Round needle file (from a jewelry supplier)

Note: *Although you may use tools that contain aluminum (such as circle cutters), avoid prolonged contact between the aluminum tool and fresh PMC because the aluminum will cause contamination.*

Universal measuring system

Decks of cards have become the universal tool for rolling even slabs of PMC to specific thicknesses. Tape together the following sets of cards: 2 sets of 2 each, 2 sets of 3 each, 2 sets of 4 each, 2 sets of 5 each, and 2 sets of 6 each. For a deep relief, a two-sided texture, or a piece you intend to carve, you can combine the card stacks: 4 and 3 to get 7 or 5 and 3 to get 8. The main drawback of using cards is that they're plastic coated and therefore slippery. Other ideas for rolling PMC to a consistent height include using strips of cardboard, using rubber gaskets, in a range of sizes, slipped on the ends

of your rolling tool, or wrapping masking tape around the ends of your rolling tools to correspond to the card system.

Making Slip

Think of slip as glue. It's what you'll use to assemble leather-hard parts and fill small cracks. You can also apply it as a surface texture. Slip needs to be thick. To test it, use the slip to attach one leather-hard piece to another, count to 10, and turn the piece upside down. Slip that's a good working consistency will hold the pieces together.

Pinch a piece of fresh PMC clay off, and put it on your work surface. Spritz it or pour a few drops of water on it, and smear it with your palette knife against the glass repeatedly. The material resists for a while, but then the two mix. The consistency you're aiming for is much thicker than paint and could be likened to frosting—that is, it holds peaks. Using distilled water will help eliminate mold in the PMC. If mold forms, just scrape it off. Save small scraps and shards to add to a slip jar.

Joining

Joining fresh PMC to fresh PMC requires a few drops of water and then a bit of smoothing over the joint until you can no longer see it. If the clay is too wet, it's beginning to crack, or you aren't making progress, put it aside to dry. When it's completely dry and easier to handle, you can add clay, fill cracks, and smooth rough areas.

Repairing Leather-Hard PMC

When making repairs, use the thickest version of PMC you can handle in the situation. If you can, use PMC right out of the package (after brushing water on the spot). If the repair is in too tight a spot, or if something else makes the thickness of PMC out of the package difficult to use, then repair it with thick slip.

Adding Texture and Embellishments

Most people's first foray into PMC involves texturing. The simple process and beautiful results make it a good place to begin.

For a rigid texture

Oil the texture. Roll out PMC to a height of 3 cards (or 4 cards for a deep relief), through plastic wrap. Lift the PMC with the plastic in place onto the oiled texture and secure it to your work surface with a small lump of polymer clay at each corner or with tape. Roll across the PMC a few times, then lift up a corner to see if it has taken a good impression. Transfer the clay to a teflon palette, texture side up, cover with plastic, and proceed with your design.

For a flexible texture

If you're using something like the plastic netting that onions come in, roll out the PMC to a height of 3 cards, transfer it to Teflon, lay the oiled netting onto the PMC, cover with plastic wrap and roll over it.

Top left: carved polymer clay plates and bottom left: clay paper, and polymer clay plate from Tear-Away technique (by Celie Fago). Right: assorted found textures. Center: drywall sanding screen.

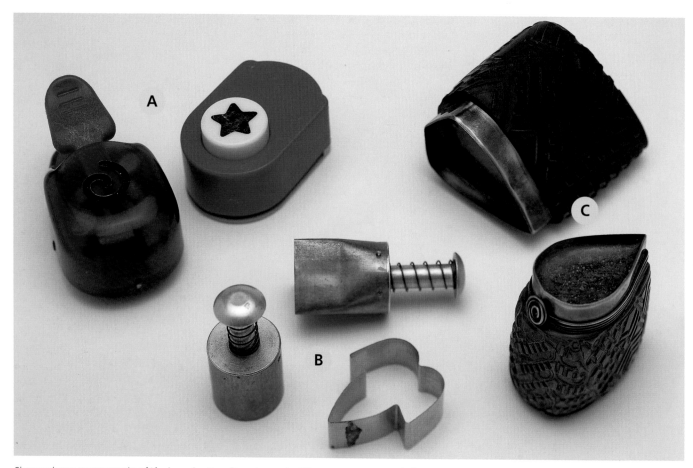

*Shown above: paper punches **(A)**, shaped cutters for polymer clay **(B)**, custom cutters made from carved polymer clay and brass (by Celie Fago) **(C)**.*

For a double-sided texture

This takes a bit of practice, but it's worth it. Because you'll be impressing both sides, start by rolling the clay out to a height of 4 cards, and if it seems too thin, go higher. It's also a good idea to choose textures with low relief. Secure the first texture to your work surface with a small lump of polymer clay (or tape) at each corner, and oil the texture well. Transfer the clay, with the plastic wrap in place, onto the first texture, and roll once or twice firmly across it. Place the second, well-oiled texture carefully on top of the clay, and roll once or twice across it. Check the impression. Two-sided texturing is much easier if the top texture is flexible. Then, it's an easy matter to check the progress of the impression by lifting up an edge.

If you don't like the way a texture looks or you change your mind and want to start over, ball up the clay you've used and spritz it lightly with water. Knead it for a few seconds through plastic, then add it back to the original ounce. Take a fresh piece from another part of the ounce to start again. Kneading the clay like this, or "wedging," is a good general strategy for getting bits of clay with different moisture levels homogenized.

Embellishments

Make the following embellishments in fresh clay, let them dry to leather-hard. Store the twisted "wires" in drinking straws and the spheres and bails sorted into plastic pill minders for later use.

Twisted "wire"

To make small twisted wires, roll out ¼ ounce of PMC, under plastic wrap, to the height of 4 cards. It should form a rectangle at least 2¼" (5.5 cm) long. Transfer the PMC to a Teflon palette. Using a well-oiled tissue blade, cut a strip as wide as the PMC is thick so that it's square. Then, take an end in each hand, and gently twist the strip. To prevent it from untwisting, firmly push both ends onto an oil-free glass surface, or another surface to which the PMC will stick, like marble or stone. Continue making twisted wires until you have enough for the project you're working on, plus a few extras in case some break. Don't worry about sizing. Just add in a little extra length, and plan on trimming the wires with a protected tissue blade once they're leather-hard. When dry, they'll detach from the glass on their own. You can

usually straighten pieces that develop a curve. Weight the leather-hard pieces under a book or store them in cocktail straws to help keep them straight. To make larger sizes of twisted wires, simply roll out a thicker slab and cut bigger square lengths of clay.

Spheres

Although there are several ways to make spheres, this one is the most efficient. Roll PMC out to a height of four cards, and with the plastic wrap in place, transfer it to a Teflon palette. Lightly oil a tube section (or a drinking straw), and press out several circles of clay. Pick one up—being careful to re-cover the others with the plastic wrap—and place it on your palm. Now roll vigorously with a finger, against your palm until you have a perfect, round sphere. Trial and error will tell you whether to add a bit of water or oil as you roll. Experiment, and try both until you can successfully roll spheres without cracks. Dry the spheres on a scrap of foam so they don't develop flat areas.

Spherical bails

After you've become proficient at rolling spheres, try the following technique for making a spherical bail. The word bail refers to that part of a piece of jewelry that connects a pendant to a chain. For the following technique to be successful, you must use copious amounts of oil. Have ready the following: a needle tool, a large wooden knitting needle (or a sharpened pencil or other large tapered tool), olive oil container, and a scrap of foam. Follow the preceding instructions for making a sphere, but start with more clay and make a larger ball. Cut a circle of clay, and roll it swiftly into a smooth ball. Place it in your palm while you oil your needle tool. Make a hole through the center of the ball using a turning and pushing motion, while spinning it against your palm. The instant you encounter resistance, re-oil the needle. Just as you reach the other side, take it out and re-oil it, and start back through from the other side, re-oiling as necessary. Now, pick up your pencil or bigger tapered tool; slather the tip with oil, and start through the hole using a turning and pushing motion, re-oiling at the first sign of resistance. Once you get the basic tool through, you can start expanding the hole diameter by rolling the ball back and forth against your palm. The key is oil. When you're satisfied with the bail, set it aside on foam to dry. Attach it with slip when it's leather-hard.

Though it's possible to do this with PMC Plus, it's more difficult. For PMC Plus, I recommend forming the sphere, letting it dry, and drilling it with a hand drill, Dremel, or flex shaft. For either material, clean up the hole in the sphere when it's leather-hard with a round needle file.

Ring Sizing

In the Ring Project, a simple technique is described for sizing a ring for a particular finger. Ring sizing is an inexact science. Ring sizes refer to several competing systems, and your finger size fluctuates over time. The following numbers assume a ring of average thickness—1/16" for small sizes and 1/8" for larger (1.5 mm for small sizes and 2 mm for larger) and a width of about 1/4" (5 mm). If your ring will be very wide, add a half a size to your calculations.

There are two ways to use the ring chart. If you have a ring sizer, find the size you want, match it to the ring sizes in the left hand column and follow it across to the type of clay you're using. If you don't have a sizer, wrap a piece of paper around the middle knuckle of the finger for which you're making a ring. That millimeter measurement is the size your ring should be after firing. Match that number to the numbers in the second from the left column (metal). Now follow across to the number in the column for PMC or PMC Plus, and cut a strip that length in fresh clay. Generally, PMC Plus is the better choice for rings.

Mandrels

A ring mandrel is a long, tapered steel tool. If your PMC ring has become misshapen during firing or it's tight on your finger, slip it onto the mandrel and tap it with a rawhide mallet.

Warpage

Once PMC is in the kiln, gravity will flatten most warps. Any additional flattening can be done after firing by placing the piece on a bench block or other flat surface and using the heel of your hand or, failing that, tapping with a rawhide or plastic mallet.

Firing

When the PMC is dry, place it on a shelf in an electric kiln. During the firing, any remaining water evaporates, the binder ignites and burns up, then the metal particles fuse together in a process called sintering. My electric kiln—designed for use with (silver) PMC—takes about 40 minutes to ramp up to the set temperature. This can vary depending on individual electrical supply. Set the temperature according to the chart shown at left.

RING CHART

Ring Size	Metal (mm)	PMC Plus (mm)	PMC (mm)
2	44.6	50.7	61.9
2 1/2	45.8	52.0	63.6
3	47.1	53.5	65.4
3 1/2	48.4	55.0	67.2
4	49.6	56.4	68.8
4 1/2	50.9	57.8	70.7
5	52.1	59.2	72.4
5 1/2	53.4	60.7	74.2
6	54.6	62.0	75.8
6 1/2	55.9	63.5	77.6
7	57.1	64.8	79.3
7 1/2	58.4	66.4	81.1
8	59.7	67.8	82.9
8 1/2	60.9	69.2	84.6
9	62.2	70.7	86.4
9 1/2	63.4	72.0	88.0
10	64.7	73.5	89.9
10 1/2	65.9	74.8	91.5
11	67.2	76.4	93.3
11 1/2	68.5	77.8	95.1
12	69.7	79.2	96.8
12 1/2	71.0	80.7	98.6
13	72.2	82.0	100.3

FIRING CHART

	temperature		time
Standard PMC – silver	1650° F	900° C	two hours
Standard PMC – gold	1830° F	1000° C	two hours
PMC Plus – silver	1650° F	900° C	10 minutes
or	1560° F	860° C	20 minutes
or	1470° F	800° C	30 minutes

Pieces ready for the kiln on a kiln shelf: top left, spherical PMC bead in a bed of vermiculite; top right, flat pieces directly on the kiln shelf; bottom right, ring on a layer of alumina hydrate; bottom left, flat piece directly on kiln shelf.

The lower temperature offers exciting possibilities that have yet to be fully explored; glass and enamel powders that will discolor at the higher temperatures will be more stable at 1470° F (799° C) and can be combined with PMC Plus.

Although the two clays can be mixed, standard PMC needs to be fired for the full 2 hours to attain maximum strength. If you mistakenly use standard slip to close a joint in a PMC Plus object, and fire it for 10 minutes; the joint will be weak. To rectify this, re-fire for a full 2 hours at 1650° F (899° C).

Any kiln that will reliably maintain the set temperature for the above duration can be used, but the ideal choice is a small kiln with a programmable thermostat and a temperature controller designed for use with PMC. Kilns designed for enameling and glass will also work.

Firing Materials

Kiln shelves

Shelves make it easier to load and empty the kiln. They also protect the floor of the kiln from meltdown accidents. Suggested materials include:

- soldering pads (depicted)—Available from jewelry supply companies, these pads are fragile but when handled carefully will last a long time.

- soft firebrick—Available from ceramic supply companies, this brick can be cut with a hack saw or jeweler's saw into 1" (3 cm) slabs (thinner will break). This brick is also good for making noncombustible support forms.

- Cordierite—This ceramic tile, available from ceramic suppliers, is a good choice for firing PMC; however, its weight limits its use to the bottom shelf.

If you're firing several pieces, you may want to stack your shelves. Stacking is safe up to 1" (3 cm) from the ceiling of the kiln. Cut up soldering pads or firebrick to make 1" (3 cm) pieces to put at each corner for stacking the shelves. Pre-made kiln posts are available from ceramic suppliers.

Leave about 1" (3 cm) of space between the edge of the shelf and the walls of the kiln, and make sure the pyrometer (heat sensor) isn't pressed against one of the shelves.

Other Kiln Furniture

Firing volumetric pieces require a little extra effort to prevent slumping. A terra-cotta dish, the kind you'd put under a potted plant, will work. Fortunately they aren't expensive because they survive only a few firings. An alternative is carving a depression in soft firebrick or molding a dish from paper clay and letting it air dry. Paper clay is a premixed paper product containing paper pulp, binder, and volcanic ash. The latter keeps it from burning up in the kiln, so paper clay shrinks very little (unlike papier mâché), making it a good choice for a noncombustible support form or for a saggar dish in which to fire volumetric forms. Fill the saggar dish with any of the following materials and nestle your beads or volumetric pieces so that about two-thirds of the bead or piece is buried (see picture).

Bedding materials

- Alumina hydrate—a fine gray-white powder used in ceramic studios (It discolors slightly with use.)

- Vermiculite—a soil additive that is a form of mica

- Plaster of Paris—plaster that can be used straight from the bag (Don't add water. If it sticks together during firing, just break it apart.)

- Investment—a material similar to plaster that is used in jewelry casting

- Loose wool—ceramic fiber material available by the pound from ceramic suppliers

- Safety note: Wear a mask when using these products, and clean up spills with a dampened paper towel, not a vacuum cleaner.

These bedding materials can be piled directly on to your kiln shelves, but they tend to spill off. When firing rings, sprinkle alumina directly onto the kiln shelf and place the ring on the layer of alumina. Contain beads and other volumetric forms in a terra-cotta dish or carved out firebrick.

Once the binder has burned away (in the first ½ hour), but before the metal particles have fused together, the PMC pieces are susceptible to gravity. Place your pieces in the dish with the heaviest part at the bottom. For example, the point of a cone should be buried in the bedding material; the open end should be up.

A little while into the kiln cycle the binder will burn up, briefly producing an odor similar to that of a spill in a hot oven. It generally last 3 to 4 minutes and is no cause for alarm. There are products, such as wax or snack food armatures

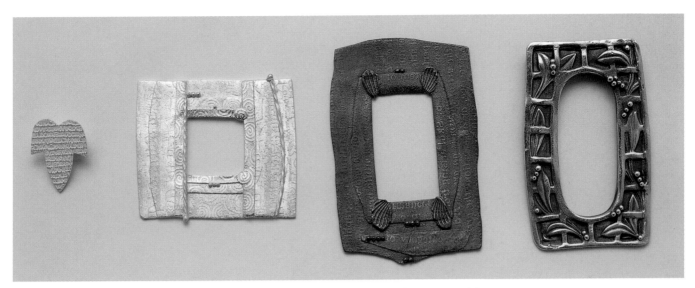

Steps in finishing PMC: from left to right, fresh from the kiln; brass brushed; blackened; highlighted by polishing.

with a high-fat content that will cause smoking during the first part of the cycle. They'll burn off harmlessly within a few minutes, but it's important to leave the kiln door closed. (Check with the PMC Guild for information on firing services.)

Cooling versus Quenching

When the kiln cycle is finished, unplug the kiln, and choose one of the following options: (1) Let the kiln sit with the door closed for several hours, or overnight. When completely cool, open the door and unload. (2) Wait 5 minutes; wearing fireproof gloves, carefully crack the door open 1" to 2" (3 cm to 5 cm). When the red glow has subsided, in 10 minutes, unload the kiln. Wear fireproof gloves and use barbecue tongs or extra-long tweezers, and either drop pieces carefully into a metal container full of water (that is, "quench" them) or transfer the pieces to a heat-proof surface and allow them to cool completely. Either technique is fine for PMC, but if your silver pieces contain synthetic gems or enamels or other materials that may be subject to thermal shock, let them air cool.

Finishing

Fresh from the kiln, all PMC pieces appear to be a matte white color. This color isn't a coating or residue, it's simply the color of the unpolished metal. The highly reflective shine usually associated with silver is the result of polishing; the color of silver is the reflection of light.

Polishing

Polishing choices occur along a continuum, with matte (right out of the kiln) at one end and shiny (or highly polished) at the other. If you looked at matte white silver under a magnifier, you'd see the top surface is made of countless peaks and valleys that trap light, creating what we know as a matte surface. Polishing smoothes out these peaks and valleys, causing light to bounce back—what we know as shine. The degree of shine and the type of finish are personal choices, but it's recommended that freshly fired pieces be polished or burnished until they no longer appear white. Fine or pure silver doesn't tarnish, but if it's left it its white state, it will trap dirt and dust and appear dingy over time.

Other polishing tools

Pieces fresh from the kiln may be scrubbed with brass or soft stainless steel bristle brush (available from jewelry suppliers). When scratch brushing, work at a sink, with the piece cradled in one hand and the brush in the other. Put dish detergent on your brush, scrub vigorously, rinsing the piece periodically so you can check progress. Continue until no trace of white is left. A scratch brush is efficient at getting into the deep relief of a design. You can use a steel burnishing tool on surfaces with no texture, but it isn't a good tool for getting into the relief of a design.

Use steel wool (0000), synthetic steel wool (000 or 0000), or a fine satin finish wheel on a bench grinder or polishing lathe (available from jewelry suppliers). Like burnishing tools, these tools may not reach into all recessed areas; however, they do produce a satin finish. A rock tumbler with stainless steel shot and specially formulated detergent is another option.

Antiquing

Antiquing involves two steps: blackening and highlighting. Use the following products with adequate ventilation, and wear rubber gloves. Liver of Sulfur, a traditional jeweler's patinating agent, is sold as a dry, yellow gravel and also as a premixed liquid. To use the gravel, mix a small piece with very hot water. Make a hook with brass or silver wire to immerse the piece for a few seconds. Rinse the piece in cold water, and repeat until you've achieved the desired color then wash piece in soapy water. The gravel must be stored in an airtight container, in the dark.

Silver Black and Black Max are acid-based proprietary solutions sold ready mixed by jewelry suppliers and, occasionally, bead stores. Dip the piece according to the directions above, or apply the solution with a brush. After rinsing, wash pieces well in soapy water and dry.

Shown here on a pine pillow: a leather-hard PMC piece partially carved, and a fired and finished carved PMC piece. Below, a leather thimble, linoleum carving tool with custom polymer clay handle (by Celie Fago), and two wood carving tools.

Highlighting

The objective of this step is to remove the black from the raised areas while leaving the black in the recessed areas to achieve a contrast in the final, polished piece. Soft or bushy tools, like a polishing cloth or steel wool, won't achieve this effectively.

A 1,200-grit micron graded (blue) polishing paper, wrapped tightly around a stick or salon board, will travel across the surface of the object but won't get into the recessed areas. The polish achieved by using this "blue" paper is shinier than steel wool, but it's still within the definition of a satin finish. For more shine, wrap a rouge or other polishing cloth tightly around a rigid stick or salon board and, after you've finished using the polishing paper, use the same technique with a rouge cloth. Wash and dry.

Carving PMC and Polymer Clay

Polymer clay must be entirely cured to carve well. To test for doneness, try carving a spiral. If the spiral breaks as you're carving, the polymer clay may need more time or a higher temperature in the oven.

The polymer clay texture plates pictured on page 81 are made from conditioned Premo polymer clay. (I prefer the metallics and pearlescents for carving.) Roll the clay out to the thickest setting on the pasta machine. Put the clay between two pieces of wax paper, and put it on a small piece of plate glass. Put another piece of plate glass on top, and put it in a preheated oven at about 275° F (135° C). After 25 minutes, increase the temperature to 285°F (141° C) for 10 minutes. The glass keeps it perfectly flat, and the wax paper keeps it from developing shiny spots against the glass.

The best tools for carving polymer clay and PMC are wood gouges. Both **V**- and **U**-gouges work well (1.5 and 2 mm). Gouges are made for linoleum and wood carving and are sold through art stores, wood-carving and print-making supply catalogs, and some polymer clay suppliers. Place the piece to be carved on to a small pine pillow or folded face towel to prevent it from sliding around.

Carving PMC

Pushing a tool through polymer clay doesn't require much effort. But because PMC has metal in it, it offers resistance to the carving tool and requires a bit more force. To protect your holding hand from the force of the carving tool, use a leather thimble (from a quilter's supply) like a catcher's mitt on one of the fingers of the hand holding the piece. Drive the tool across the surface of the PMC into the finger that's wearing the thimble.

Standard PMC, because it has more binder in it, carves cleanly, without chipping. PMC Plus, because of its higher silver content, is a bit more challenging to carve.

Combining PMC and Polymer Clay

There are many ways to combine the two materials featured in this book. Scrap polymer clay can be used as a rehearsal material. Practice making a form in polymer clay and when you like it, re-create it in PMC. When you're pleased with a particular form in polymer clay, bake it, then put it on a copier or scanner bed, and reduce it 28% or 12% (depending on whether you're using standard PMC or PMC Plus) to get an idea of the after firing size. These 3-dimensional sketches are a great design tool that will help you visualize the end result. You can use a lump of scrap polymer clay pressed onto a corner of your work surface to anchor a wooden stake for drying a PMC bead on the other end. Aesthetically, the two materials make a unique and lovely combination. Fired and finished, PMC offers an aesthetic counterpoint to the resonant color of polymer clay.

Using Tear-Away Clay Papers to Texture PMC

1. Roll out PMC to a height of 3 cards, and place it on a Teflon palette. Lay well-oiled clay papers onto PMC, and roll it into the PMC through plastic wrap.

2. Gently peel off the paper. Don't be surprised if some of the polymer clay remains on the surface of the PMC. Tear-away clay paper is fragile and will yield only a few impressions, but while it lasts, it creates a lovely surface texture.

Using a Tear-Away Etched Polymer Clay Plate to Texture PMC

The polymer clay portion of the Tear-Away is a bit more durable. You'll get many good impressions from one plate.

1. Secure the polymer clay plate to your work surface using masking tape or balls of scrap polymer clay, and oil the plate well.

2. Roll PMC out to a height of 3 cards, and lay it onto the polymer clay. Gently and firmly roll once across the surface. If you aren't happy with the impression, ball up the clay and try again.

There are numerous ways to combine PMC and polymer clay. You can work thinly and economically in the metal clay with the intention of adding a decorative backing in polymer clay. Silver bezels or frames around polymer clay are a lovely and traditional way to complement both materials, as are polymer clay buttons that contain PMC as a decorative or structural addition. Mastering rings in PMC teaches you to make cylindrical forms. Working in polymer clay offers many opportunities to use silver cylindrical forms. You can use them as ornaments on bracelets (see gallery), as a starting point for necklace terminations such as cord ends, and as a base for polymer clay inlay. You'll discover your own possibilities for invention in this material once you master a few basics.

Although it's possible to duplicate many conventional metal-fabrication techniques using PMC, the vestigial clay character in finished PMC works accounts for a great deal of its charm.

TEAR-AWAY TECHNIQUE FOR POLYMER CLAY

Polymer Clay

Originally developed for polymer clay by Gwen Gibson and adapted here by Celie Fago,* the tear-away technique offers a unique way to texture PMC or polymer clay by creating etched plates and clay papers from photocopies of your collages, designs, or copyright-free artwork. The process consists of burnishing a photocopy onto polymer clay, resting it, and then tearing it away. Because the photocopy toner bonds with the clay, the paper brings a layer of clay with it when it's torn away. Once baked, this "clay paper" becomes a lovely, delicate texturing tool. The clay the paper has been torn from is impressed with a delicate relief of the image from the photocopy. When it's baked, it becomes a durable texturing "plate."

STEPS

1. Roll out conditioned polymer clay to a number 1 or 2 on your pasta machine (use thickest or next-to-the-thickest setting). Cut a piece a bit larger than your intended image, and place it on a portable surface that can go into the oven—for example, plate glass, an oven tray, or wax paper.

2. Place the photocopy face down on the clay, and fold a corner up to use as a tab. Burnish the copy onto the clay

using a circular motion, first with your fist and then with the bone folder, for about a minute.

3. Position the piece 6" to 8" (15 cm to 20 cm) under a lamp, and let it rest for about 7 minutes. Burnish it for 1 minute, and then let it rest again under the lamp for another 7 minutes.

Tip: Experiment with the variables: heat, time, friction, different clay brands (I've had good luck with Sculpey III) and photocopies. Too little heat, or friction, and nothing happens; too much heat, and the photocopy image transfers to the clay.

4. Holding the surface steady with one hand, grasp the paper tab, and tear the paper off the clay. For best results, tear low and quickly, in one smooth motion. Bake the etched clay plate and the paper portion, which will be rolled up, according to manufacturer's instructions. Wait until after baking to unroll the clay paper.

The 'clay paper' can be unrolled and flattened out and used as a collage element or as a picture in itself, or it can be used as a texturing tool for PMC or polymer clay. The etched clay plate can be used for texturing as well. You can also rub acrylic or oil paint into the etched surface for a scrimshaw-like effect, buff it up when the paint is dry, and use it as a picture or a pin.

* For further study, see Gwen's video *Ancient Images*. See the resources section for more information.

Creating with Precious Metal Clay

The following projects are designed to demonstrate the range of possibilities of Precious Metal Clay (PMC), an array of different techniques, and how to successfully combine polymer clay and PMC. Each project also provides general skills and specific tips with the idea that you'll ultimately transform this information to suit your own working style.

The maple leaf earrings (on page 102) not only illustrate the use of texture but the concept of using shrinkage as part of composition. The ring project (on page 94) provides an easy method of sizing rings and closing joints and introduces simple, elegant ways to use PMC Sheet. Beauty and function combine in the toggle clasp project (on page 90), which can add a personal touch to an old necklace or complement and complete one of your own creations. The frame project (on page 106) is a wonderful example of the marriage between polymer clay and Precious Metal Clay; it uses polymer as a texture, as an image to frame, and as a decorative support for the frame itself. The celestial spheres project (on page 98) shows you how to create a hollow form bead using a combustible core and then applique small embellishments onto the bead. The box pendant (on page 110) is a more challenging project. It teaches precision, the use of noncombustible support forms, and the challenges of working with leather-hard PMC.

These projects are meant as a starting point: Experiment as you work, and don't be discouraged by mistakes, because you'll make discoveries, as well. Remember, PMC is a new material—and the possibilities are truly limitless.

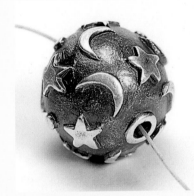

Carved Circle and Bar Toggle

Artist: Celie Fago

PMC allows you the freedom to design a unique toggle any scale or size to fit a particular design—from a delicate bracelet toggle to a bold design for a large bead necklace. The toggle seen here is a carved bar and circle made from PMC Plus. In a complex design, just as in a simple one, you'll need to consider how a toggle functions: The bar piece needs to be long enough to be securely captured by the circle piece. You can study the proportions of commercial toggle clasps in a jewelry catalog or you can make a working model from polymer clay to better understand how a particular design will work in a specific setting. A beautiful toggle can also be the centerpiece for a necklace.

Materials

- basic Precious Metal Clay equipment and supplies (see page 80)
- 1 sheet copy paper
- 1 package of PMC Plus
- 2 large jump rings
- photocopier
- foam rubber scraps
- chain nose pliers
- carving tool (2 mm **V**-gouge Micro Carving Tool or your choice)
- hand towel or small pine sachet pillow
- hand drill with a $1/16$" (1.5 mm) drill bit (or a Dremel or flex shaft)
- round needle file

Getting Started

When drying rounded shapes, place them on foam rubber and turn them over every 10 to 15 minutes so that they don't develop a flat side.

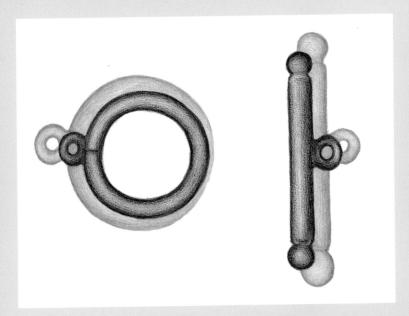

1 Determine the size you want your toggle to be.

Make a simple rendition of a circle and a bar that size, on paper. If three-dimensional "sketching" works better for you, make and bake a bar and circle in polymer clay the size you want your toggle to be. Copy the paper or the polymer clay "sketch" at 115 percent. This is the size you need to make the toggle using fresh PMC Plus to compensate for 12 percent shrinkage that occurs during firing.

2 Form the toggle.

To make the featured toggle, first roll ½ package of PMC Plus into a rope about ¼" (6 mm) in diameter with a rolling rectangle. Don't use oil, but if the clay begins to dry out, tent it with plastic wrap as you roll. (See *Tools* and *Rolling Techniques* on pages 78-80.)

Next, cut a section about 2¾" (70 mm) long, and cut a bevel on each end. Brush water on each end, and form it into a circle so the beveled ends match up, smoothing the joint well with an oiled finger or a brush. Remember that you can add clay to the joint once it's leather-hard or sand any excess clay away, so concentrate on getting the beveled ends attached so the circle so it will hold its shape while drying. Lay the circle on a piece of foam rubber to dry.

To make the bar, cut another section of the rope about 1¼" (30 mm) long and set it on foam rubber to dry.

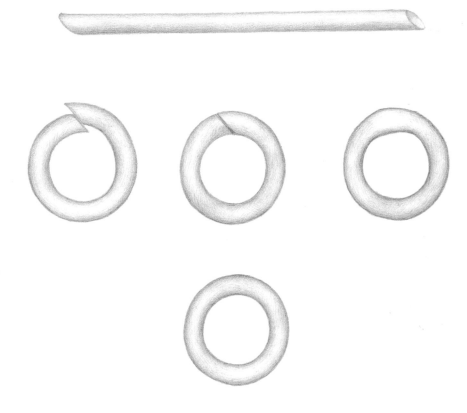

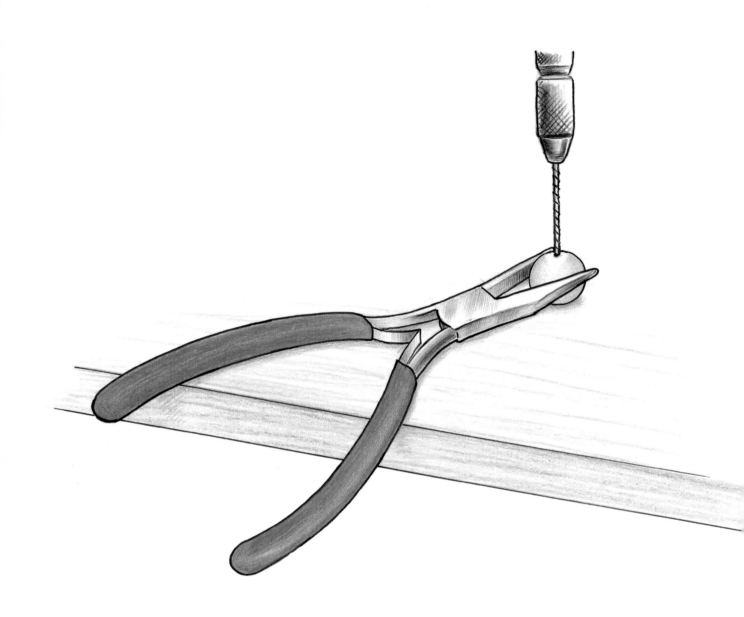

3 Make the decorative spheres for the toggle.

Cut four more segments from the PMC Plus rope, each about 4 mm long, and roll them into balls. (For other methods, see *Embellishments* on page 82.) Set the balls on foam rubber, and allow them to completely dry. Then, holding the balls flat on a table and firmly in the jaws of chain nose pliers, drill holes through two of the balls with a ¹⁄₁₆" (1.5 mm) drill bit, a Dremel or a flex shaft, to accommodate the jump rings that will be used to attach the toggle to a chain. (Image shown features a larger bead; actual sphere for this project is smaller.) Clean up the holes with a round needle file. Refine the circle and bar with nail boards and/or sandpaper (320, 400, then 600 grit), and fill any cracks with slip. If there are large cracks, brush them with water, and then push PMC Plus right out of the package into the cracks.

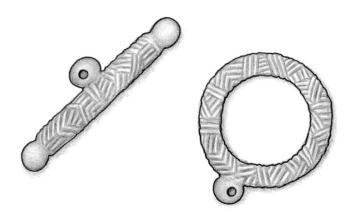

4 Carve the toggle pieces.

The featured toggle was carved using a **V**-gouge Micro-Carving tool, which was designed for carving wood. It's helpful to nestle the piece to be carved onto a folded hand towel or a small pine or sachet pillow. This will keep it from sliding around and also cushion it to prevent breakage. (See *Carving* on page 86.)

5 Attach the leather-hard pieces.

See *Making Slip* on page 81. Affix the two undrilled balls to the ends of the carved bar. Attach one of the balls with a hole to the middle of the bar as seen here, and set it aside to dry. Then, attach the other drilled ball to the outer edge of the carved circle, as seen here, and set it aside to dry. These attachments need to be well secured with thick slip, checked for gaps when dry, and refilled where necessary to ensure a structurally sound toggle. Fire flat on a bed of alumina hydrate or vermiculite. (See *Firing* on page 83.) Scrub with a brass brush, and finish as desired. Finally, attach the toggle to a necklace or bracelet using jump rings.

Variations

The toggle on the left was carved using the method described above. The wiggling snake functions as the bar in this variation. The snake with its tail in its mouth, an age-old symbol of infinity, serves the function of the circle. The heart and arrow toggle is made from clay that has been textured on both sides and cut out with a heart-shaped cookie cutter. The arrow shape was cut by hand with an oiled tissue blade.

PMC Appliqué Ring

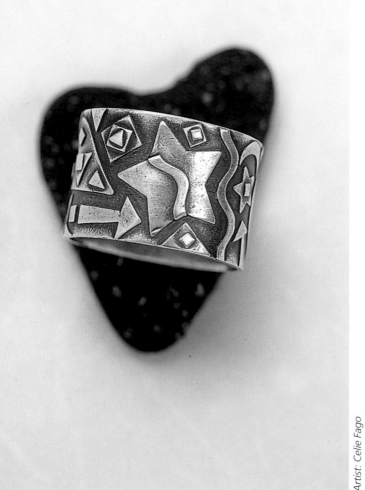

Artist: Celie Fago

PMC Sheet opens up a whole new realm of design possibilities. Paper-cutting tools, such as punches and edgers, create stylish designs simply and easily. There is a vast array of patterns and motifs available in these craft cutters. You can make your design unique by cutting freehand details such as triangles or arrows to add to your ring, using a craft knife, a protected tissue blade, or a wavy blade. Try a design by cutting shapes from copy paper first. When you're satisfied, proceed to the PMC Sheet.

Materials

- basic Precious Metal Clay equipment and supplies (see page 80)
- copy paper
- clear tape
- 1 package PMC Plus
- 1 PMC Sheet
- paper scissors
- paper punches in assorted shapes, such as a star, moon, or spiral
- ripple or wavy blade
- ring mandrel
- rawhide or plastic mallet
- brass brush

Getting Started

If you have trouble with the PMC Plus sticking to your work surface, try rolling directly on a piece of Teflon taped to your work surface. Remember to flip the clay over every three or four rolls, which will help minimize sticking.

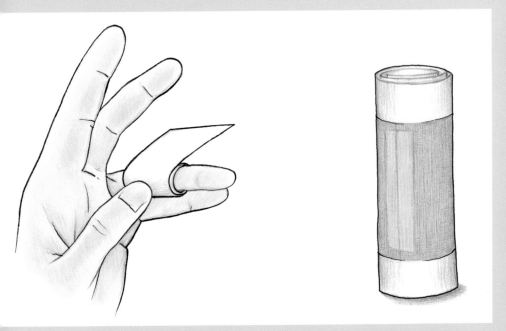

1 Make the ring form.

Cut a piece of copy paper into a rectangle about 3½" x 1¾" (9 cm x 5 cm). Wrap the paper around the middle knuckle of the finger for which you want to make a ring, then use clear tape to close it. This is the size you want your ring to be after firing. Since PMC Plus shrinks 12 percent during firing, it's necessary to add a millimeter of thickness to the ring form. To do this, cut two or three strips of paper and wrap them around the ring form while it's on your finger. It will take seven revolutions of copy paper to add the needed thickness. Next, wrap the whole thing with a piece of Teflon paper, then use clear tape to close it. If you're have trouble getting the paper strips tight, try wrapping the paper form with masking tape instead of paper. (See *Ring Sizing* on page 83 for alternative methods.)

2 Form the ring.

Wrap a small scrap of paper around your ring form to measure the circumference, then lay the paper flat on your work surface to use as a length guide. Lightly oil the work surface, and roll out ½ a package of PMC Plus, through plastic wrap, to a height of three cards. Using a well-oiled tissue blade, cut the PMC Plus into a strip slightly wider than you want your finished ring to be and approximately ¼" (6 mm) longer than the paper guide. The featured ring was rolled out to a height of three cards, and cut to a width of ⅝" (16 mm). Next, cut one end of the PMC strip at a blunt right angle.

Next, wrap the PMC strip around the Teflon-covered paper form, and overlap the ends. Try not to stretch the clay. Using an oiled tissue blade, cut through the two layers of PMC at an angle in one smooth motion so that both ends are beveled. Gently lift the top layer of PMC, and remove the excess clay from the bottom layer. Abut the two beveled ends, and seal the joint with a few drops of water. Smooth the joint to seal it well using an oiled finger, a brush, or similar tool.

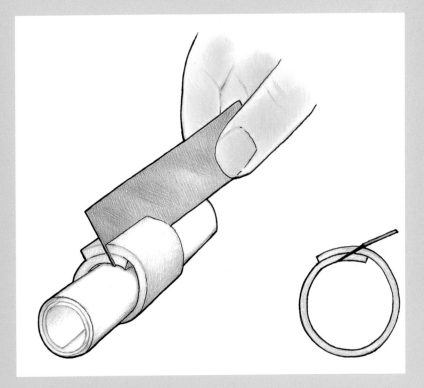

3 Dry the ring.

As the clay dries to leather-hard, it will lose moisture and shrink slightly. Sometimes this is just enough shrinkage to force open a weak joint. Monitor the drying, and after 15 minutes or so, carefully slide the ring off the form and place it upright, in a safe spot to dry. The easiest way to do this is to slide the teflon off with the ring in place. Then use tweezers to grasp the Teflon strip inside the ring and, with a half turn inward, pull the Teflon out. Now, place the upright ring in a safe place to dry. If the joint opens or your ring develops other cracks, fill them with thick slip. Make sure all parts of the ring are completely dry before repairing anything.

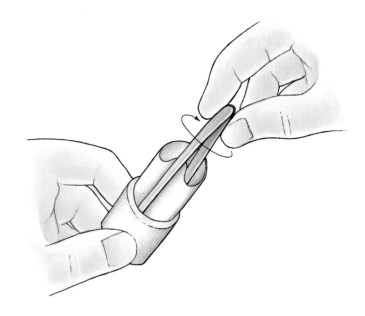

4 Sand and level the ring.

When the ring is dry, sand and true up as necessary. To true up your ring, slide it back onto the paper form after removing one or two layers of paper so there is still a snug fit. Position the ring so that it is protruding slightly off the end of the paper form. Sand it on a piece of medium-fine sandpaper (400- or 320-grit) laid flat on a piece of glass or other flat surface. Sand both edges in this way, then smooth any flaws in the rest of the ring. Smooth the inside by rolling a piece of 400-grit sandpaper to a size that moves freely in the ring. Proceed to 600-grit and then to 1000-grit if desired. Set aside.

5 Decorate the ring.

Using hand punches, cut out spirals, hearts, or other shapes from the PMC Sheet. Shapes can also be cut freehand using a craft knife or a protected tissue blade to make your ring design unique. Cut strips from the PMC Sheet with a wavy blade to complement your design. To attach the cut pieces to the ring, lay the shape in the desired place, then run a bead of water around it using a paintbrush. Press gently to attach. Another way to attach the cut pieces is to dampen a spot on the ring and press the piece onto the wet area. If the piece becomes too moist, or if you try to move it once it has been attached with water, it will tear.

6 Fire the ring.

Fire the ring upright on a kiln shelf that has been sprinkled with alumina hydrate. The alumina will reduce friction as the ring shrinks and ensure that it doesn't end up bigger on the bottom than the top. If it does become misshapen in the kiln, you can tap it back in to shape by slipping it onto a ring mandrel and tapping it with a rawhide or plastic mallet. (See *Firing* on page 83.) Scrub with a brass brush, and finish as desired.

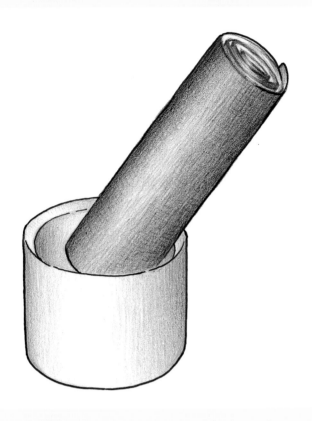

TIP: BEVEL THE INSIDE EDGES OF THE RING.

After sanding and leveling, beveling the inside edges of the ring will allow it to slide smoothly on and off your finger and will make it look more finished and more professional. To do this, roll up a piece of 400-grit sandpaper so it can move freely in and out of the inside of the ring at an acute angle. Then, sand using a gentle back and forth motion while turning the ring. Be sure to bevel both sides of the ring.

Variations

Freehand Designs and Texturing.

Cut a strip of PMC Sheet, long enough to encircle your leather-hard ring. Using a craft knife with a new blade, cut out a pattern of interior shapes. The featured ring on the top shows a pattern of leaf shapes that were cut using this method. You can practice your design on a sheet of paper. If your ring's circumference is greater than the length of the PMC Sheet, use two or more sections to encircle the ring, making the seams a part of the design or abutting the ends, letting it dry and carefully filling in the seams with slip until they are invisible.

Follow the directions for making the ring described in the main project. Then, to adhere the strip to the leather-hard ring, first quickly paint the ring with medium-thin, lump-free slip. Let the ring dry and reinforce any gaps as necessary with slip or water. Fire, scrub with a brass brush, and finish.

The cut-out shapes on this ring (bottom) were attached to a leather-hard textured ring. Once fired, the cut-outs fuse to and take on the shape of the ring's surface, adding an additional element of texture and dimension.

TIP

To make thicker paper, which creates a more dramatic relief for your ring design, spray one PMC Sheet with a fine mist of water. Wait 5 seconds then place a second PMC Sheet on top, and press gently. Allow to dry, then use it as you would any PMC Sheet.

Celestial Sphere Beads

In this project you'll use found core materials to make round, hollow form beads. The smaller bead pictured was made by using a round piece of cereal as a core. The cereal is painted with white glue and covered with a layer of PMC. When it's dried, the bead is embellished with designs in fresh PMC. Round cereal, puffed corn, or round snack foods make good core materials for spherical beads. This project uses a cereal core of an average diameter of 10 cm. Adjust the numbers for other combustible cores. Fresh or freeze-dried cranberries also work but with any food that contains water it's important to apply a quick coat of acrylic gel medium as a moisture barrier and let it dry before you begin.

Artist: Celie Fago

Materials

- basic Precious Metal Clay equipment and supplies (see page 80)
- small combustible cores, such as round cereal
- scrap polymer clay
- 1 package of PMC Plus
- small brass tube or small straw
- square-ended tool (small ruler)
- wire cutters

Getting Started

To sand a round shape without developing any flattened areas, fold the sandpaper to form a curved trough. Then, sand using a back-and-forth motion, and rotate the object frequently in the trough.

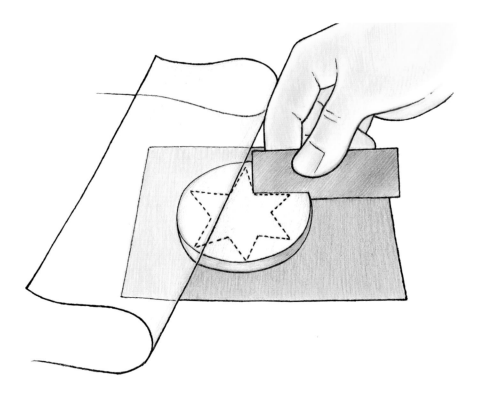

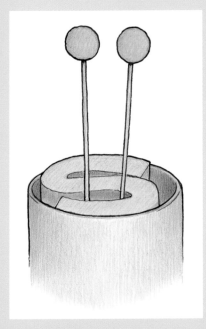

1 Prepare the bead cores.

Choose two relatively round balls for the bead cores. Make handles for them by poking a wooden skewer into each one. Apply a light coat of white craft glue to the cores, which will help adhere the PMC. Insert each skewer into a ball of scrap polymer clay pressed onto the edge of your work surface, within easy reach. Or, set the skewers into a glass with a piece of ½" (1 cm) foam rubber accordion-folded and stuffed inside. Roll out approximately ⅓ ounce of PMC Plus, through plastic wrap, to the height of three cards. Transfer the clay, with the plastic wrap in place, to a Teflon palette.

2 Covering the cores.

Lift the plastic sheet and cut a circle for each core, about 32 mm in diameter. (You may want to use an oiled plastic circle template laid on the clay. If so, cut around the circle with an oiled pin tool.) Use a tissue blade or a knife to cut a star shape out of each circle, visualizing the size of the ball you want to encase as you work. You may want to practice this technique once or twice with polymer clay. Using an oiled tissue blade or palette knife, carefully transfer one of the star shapes onto a glue-coated core. Be sure to cover the second circle with plastic wrap. Twist and remove the wood skewer from the core. Press the clay onto the core, starting from the top and working your way around. Press out air bubbles as you go. Smooth the seams together first with a little bit of water from the end of your watercolor brush, then with a lightly oiled finger. Close all the "darts" and smooth the resulting seams. Don't worry about covering the hole; it can be reopened later. You may stretch the PMC slightly, trim any excess with the tissue blade, or add more clay as needed. When all the seams are closed and the core is entirely covered, roll it vigorously between your palms to transform it from a lumpy mass into a lovely sphere. Insert the wooden skewer again, gently poking a new hole if the first one is covered. Roll the bead again between your palms until smooth. Set it aside, into the ball of polymer clay, and let dry.

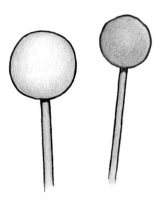

Repeat the process to make a second sphere, and let dry. Once dry, fill any cracks with thick slip. If the cracks are large, dab with water and use clay right from the package to smear into the cracks. When the repaired areas are dry, refine the shape of the beads with 400- to 600-grit sandpaper that has been folded into a curved trough. Then, with the bead resting on your work surface, position a hand drill with a ¹⁄₁₆" (1.5 mm) drill bit into the existing hole, and drill straight down through the bead to the opposite side.

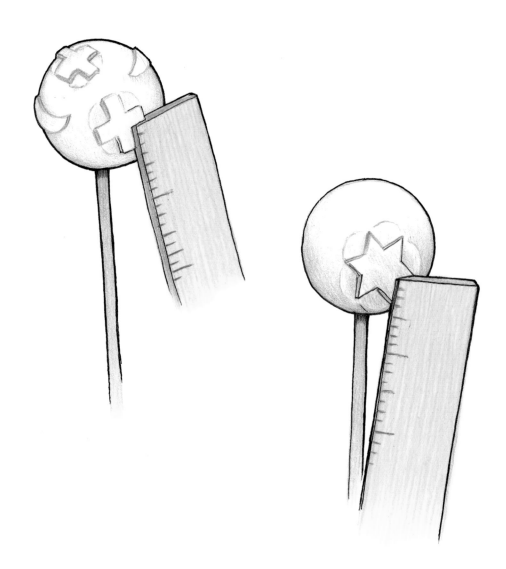

3 Decorate the spheres.

Roll out an almond-size bit of PMC, through plastic wrap, to a height of two cards. Transfer it to a Teflon palette leaving the plastic in place. Using the end of a lightly oiled small brass tube or small straw, cut out several circles of clay. Pick a spot on the sphere, and moisten it with a little water from the end of your pointed brush, then transfer a circle to the wet spot. Press to attach. Now convert the circle, and subsequent circles, into other shapes—such as a star, plus sign, or cross—by pressing a square-ended tool repeatedly around the circle. To make a star, press the tool five times around the circle, evenly spaced. To make a plus sign, press the tool four times around the circle, evenly spaced. To make a crescent moon, press the tube or straw into the PMC again, off-setting it slightly. To make a dough-nut, transfer a circle to a dry spot on the sphere, and immediately press a smaller circle into the middle of the first circle. The center should come out readily with a slight twist of the tube. Now run a bead of water around the outside edge of the doughnut and use gentle pressure to attach it. Continue adding shapes until you're satisfied with your sphere beads, then let dry.

4 Fire and finish.

Once the beads are dry, remove the skewers. If the skewers don't come out readily, cut off the ends with wire cutters so the ends are flush with the surface of the beads. The remaining wood left inside will burn out harmlessly during firing. Then, nestle the spheres into a bed of vermiculite or alumina hydrate in an unglazed ceramic dish. Leave the top third or so of the spheres protruding above the surface of the vermiculite or alumina hydrate. Put the dish onto a shelf in the kiln, and fire at any of the three firing choices for PMC Plus. (See *Firing* on page 83.) Scrub with a brass brush, and finish as desired. (See more on finishing on page 85.)

Variations

Embellishing with shards and slip.

Try using shards left over from other projects, such as the carved toggle on page 90, to decorate beads. Follow the directions for making beads described above, let them dry, then refine them. Gather leftover shards onto a piece of plastic wrap. Paint the bead with thick slip, then gently roll it in the pile of shards, guiding it along with the skewer handle. It's easy to fill in any bare spots later, when the bead is leather-hard—just paint the bare areas with thick slip, and fill with more shards. Dry and fire as directed in the main project. You can also combine shards and appliqué pieces in one design. To learn about other types of appliqué, see the ring project on page 94.

To make slip-covered beads, follow the directions for making beads described above, let them dry, then refine them. Then, paint thick, lumpy, slip over the beads until you are satisfied with the surface design. The best effects are achieved with very thick slip.

Maple Leaf Earrings

This project demonstrates the concept of relative shrinkage. Using the same-sized cutter or template to cut out both the PMC and the polymer part of this project illustrates the 28% shrinkage of standard PMC. As it happens, the relative proportions (the polymer at full size and the PMC shrunk by 28%) work very well together in finished jewelry. If you are using PMC Plus, the shrinkage is only 12%, so the PMC will be larger relative to the polymer piece, but still proportionately balanced. Both the PMC and the polymer shapes in this project were cut with a commercially available leaf-shaped cutter.

Artist: Celie Fago

Materials

- basic Precious Metal Clay equipment and supplies (see page 80)
- basic polymer clay equipment and supplies (see page 10)
- standard PMC
- texturing materials
- conditioned polymer clay in 3 or 4 colors
- scrap polymer clay
- pair of large loop earwires
- chain-nose pliers
- cutter or template of your choice, oiled
- ring mandrel or other hard, round form
- rawhide mallet
- drinking glass or ceramic coffee mug
- soft cloth or polishing lathe for polymer clay

Getting Started

If you are using a rigid texture, put the PMC onto the oiled texture. With netting or other flexible texture, it is easier to put the texture on top of the PMC. First, roll the clay out and transfer it to a piece of Teflon. Then, lay the oiled flexible texture on the clay, and go over it with a roller.

1 Texture the PMC.

Roll out PMC, through a sheet of plastic wrap, to a height of three cards. With the plastic in place, lift the PMC, gently position it on the oiled texture. Roll over the clay firmly once or twice, through the plastic, with your roller. Lift a corner, and if the PMC has taken a good impression, transfer it to teflon paper, with the textured side up. See *Texturing* on page 81.

2 Cut out the earring shapes.

Cut your chosen earring shape out with an oiled cutter. To cut a freehand design, use an oiled tissue blade. To use a plastic template, make sure it's well oiled, then lay it on the clay and trace around the shape with a pin tool. Repeat to make a second shape. Set the shapes aside to dry.

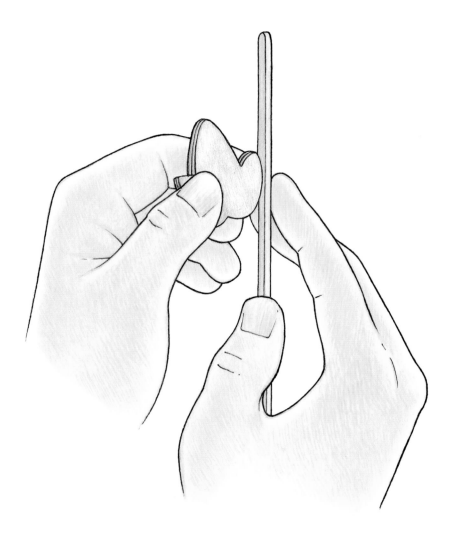

3 Refine the shape of the earrings.

Once the PMC is leather-hard, hold the two earrings together and run a nail board or sandpaper, held perpendicular to the outside edge to refine, and to match, the two shapes. Using a hand drill with a ¹⁄₁₆" (1.5 mm) drill bit, make a hole in both shapes near the tops. Make sure you leave enough distance between the hole and the edge of the earrings so that after firing and shrinking it will not be weak. For the featured maple leaf shape, the hole should be ⅛" (3 mm) from the top edge of the earring. Dry the shapes.

4 Fire the earrings.

See *Firing* on page 83. Fire flat on the kiln shelf. Unload the kiln following the usual procedure, and scrub with a brass brush (see *Polishing* on page 85). Then, lay the earrings over a curved surface such as a ring mandrel (available from jewelry supply companies). If you don't have a ring mandrel, use a dowel or your PVC roller. Gently push the pieces into a curve against the mandrel, or tap with a rawhide mallet. Repeat with second shape. Finish as desired.

5 Make the polymer clay elements.

To make textured polymer clay elements, first use a pasta machine to roll out half a block of conditioned polymer clay on setting #3 (medium thick). If you aren't texturing, roll out the clay on setting #4. Sprinkle baby powder or cornstarch on both sides of the clay sheets to prevent it from sticking to your texture or to your rolling tool. Then, lay the polymer onto the texture, and roll over it once firmly. Lift a corner; if the texture looks good, transfer the polymer clay to your work surface or waxed paper, and cut out two earring shapes with the same cutter used to cut the PMC pieces. The featured earrings were made by conditioning pearl blue, gold, copper, and a little bit of black Premo polymer clay separately, then rolling them out together. This multi-colored sheet was then textured with a carved polymer clay texture plate (see page 81).

You may bake the shapes flat or, if a curve is desired, put a drinking glass or coffee cup on its side on a baking try. Balls of scrap clay strategically positioned on either side of the glass will keep it from sliding around on the tray. Gently press the earring shapes on to the glass. If the amount of powder residue on the earring backs prevents them from sticking, put a smidgen of hand lotion on the tip of your finger and wipe the powder off the back of the earrings and try again. Bake according to manufacturer's directions. The low heat needed to bake the polymer clay won't affect the glass. Once the pieces have cooled, sand them with 600-grit and then 1,000-grit sandpaper, if desired. Buff with a cloth or on a polishing lathe set up for polymer clay. Drill a hole with a 1⁄16" (1.5 mm) drill bit near the top of the pieces. Finally, assemble the earrings by threading the earwires through a PMC and a polymer clay piece.

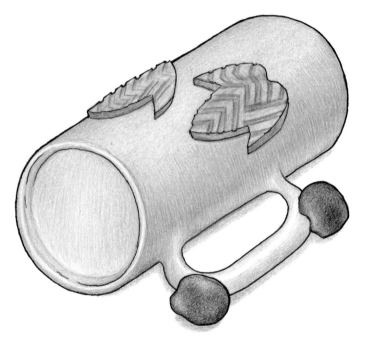

TIP

Put an extra piece of clay, the same brand and thickness as your earrings, in the oven for the duration of the baking cycle. When it's cool, try to break the extra piece. If it breaks, you know your earrings need to bake longer or at a higher temperature. Experiment with these two variables to make durable earrings.

Variations

These earrings were cut out with a custom-made tool. The tool was made by bending 24-gauge brass sheet into a leaf shape and then baking it in a polymer clay handle. The handle was then sanded and carved. Try pressing a small metal cookie cutter into a ball of polymer clay. Bake it according to manufacturer's directions, sand, and then carve it. The leaf earrings pictured were made with Premo clay and carved with a 1.5 mm **V**-gouge, micro-carving tool.

Textured Silver Frame with Inset

Artist: Celie Fago; Photo: Robert Diamante

This delicate silver frame can be used to house a small photo, or a beautiful polymer clay image, as seen here. There are many ways to texture and embellish a frame like this, and it can easily be transformed into a pendant or a brooch. Be sure to read Embellishments *on page 82 for ideas and inspiration when designing your own frame. Also, try experimenting with different frame shapes, finishes, and polymer clay transferring techniques—the possibilities are endless. The spiral image on the featured frame was made using a collage transfer and the Tear-Away technique.*

Materials

- basic Precious Metal Clay equipment and supplies (see page 80)
- basic polymer clay equipment and supplies (see page 10)
- 1 ounce of standard PMC
- Tear-Away etched plate, clay paper, or other texture, oiled
- 1 block of black polymer clay (featured piece was backed with Premo)
- image for transfer
- texture, such as sanding screen, for back of frame
- Translucent Liquid Sculpey (TLS)
- 3" (8 cm) length of 14- or 16-gauge brass, steel, or sterling wire
- five-minute epoxy
- cotton batting
- bench block or other metal surface
- hammer
- use frame templates on page 124

Getting Started

Virtually any black-and-white line drawing can be easily transferred to polymer clay (see page 17 for transfer techniques). Repeating the motifs from the picture in the frame creates a resonance that unifies these two materials. You can do this with transfer techniques and Tear-Away, by making embellishments for the frame that match the image, or by carving patterns from the image onto the frame when it's leather-hard. For carving PMC you'll need to make it extra thick because you'll be cutting into it with the carving tool.

1 Make the PMC frame.

Roll out standard PMC, through plastic wrap, to a height of three cards, nudging it into a rectangle as you go. If you're making a piece larger than 2" x 2" (5 cm x 5 cm) roll the PMC to a height of four cards. Transfer the rectangle to a Teflon palette keeping the plastic wrap in place.

2 Texture the PMC.

First, see *Using Tear-Away Plates and Clay Papers to Texture PMC* on page 87. Then, make an etched polymer plate using the Tear-Away technique. Secure the etched plate to your work surface with some scrap polymer clay at each corner. Oil the etched plate, and lay the PMC over the top, leaving the plastic wrap in place. Roll once firmly across the surface to impress, then lift the PMC to check the impression. Roll over the PMC again if necessary. Then, remove the plastic, and turn the PMC over onto to the Teflon palette, texture side up.

3 Cut out the frame opening.

Using an oiled craft knife, cut an opening in the center of the frame. Trim the outside edges of the frame and position those pieces around the opening, or trim and position only two of the outside edges, leaving the other two as is. Attach the trimmed pieces to the frame with a few drops of water. Let the frame dry.

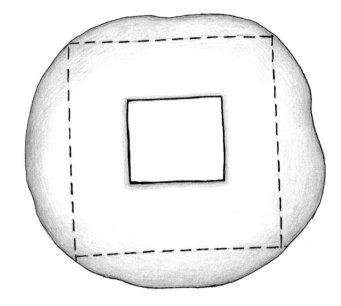

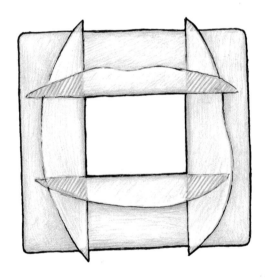

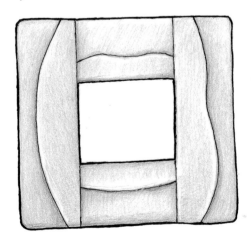

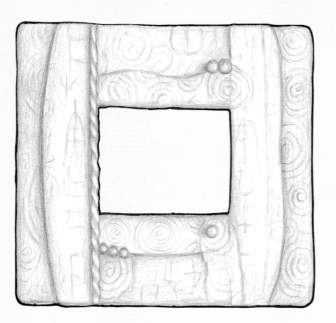

4 Decorate the surface.

Once the frame is leather-hard, check for gaps in your attachments, and reaffix with thick slip. Decorate the surface with small balls of clay and lengths of twisted PMC strips. Attach the embellishments with thick slip. (See *Embellishments* on page 82 and Step 2 in the following project.) Once the slip has dried, refine the form with a nail board or fine-grit sandpaper. Fill any cracks, gaps or weak joints with thick slip. Let dry.

5 Fire the frame.

Fire the piece flat on the kiln shelf (see *Firing* on page 83). Brass brush, antique and polish the surface as desired. Scrub the back of the frame well with steel wool, sandpaper, or a brass brush until glistening clean in preparation for gluing. (See *Finishing Techniques* on page 85.)

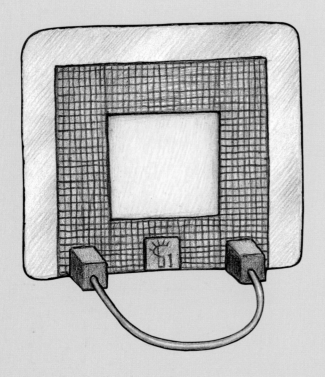

6 Make the polymer clay inset.

Transfer an image that will fit in your frame's window to a piece of rolled out polymer clay. Lay the polymer clay on a baking surface with the transfer facing up. Lower the PMC frame onto the polymer clay so the opening frames the transferred image. Press down gently to secure. Turn the piece over, and use a craft knife or tissue blade to trim the polymer clay so it s ⅛" to ¼" (3 mm to 6 mm) larger than the frame opening.

To create a finished look on the back side of the frame, first roll out some polymer clay to about the height of the transfer inset. Texture the surface as desired. Drywall sanding screen was used here. Using a tissue blade, cut thin strips from the clay sheet, long enough to enclose the back of the transfer inset. Apply TLS to the edges of the transfer inset, and abut the textured strips to make a frame. To make a spot to sign or carve your name, cut out a ½" (1 cm) long square from the middle of the bottom strip. Flip it over so the smooth side is facing up. Dab the edges with TLS and reposition it in the same spot. Make sure the bottom strip extends to the bottom edge of the PMC frame.

Next, make two ⅜" (10 mm) square cubes of polymer clay. Use a 3" (8 cm) wire to poke a hole about halfway into one side of each cube. Position the hole one-third of the way up from the bottom of the cube. Then, position the cube along the bottom edge of the polymer clay strip, and affix with TLS. Bake the entire frame assemblage on cotton batting, face down, according to the polymer clay manufacturer's directions. Let cool. Sand polymer if desired.

To assemble the frame, first use a craft knife or needle tool to roughen all surfaces to be glued—the part of the frame back and the part of the polymer piece that will be glued to each other. Then clean all surfaces by swabbing with alcohol. Prepare five-minute epoxy according to manufacturer's instructions. Glue polymer clay assemblage to the back of the PMC frame. To make the frame stand, bend the 3" (8 cm) wire into a **U**-shape loop, and poke the ends into the holes in each cube. If the wire ends don't fit snugly, remove and place them on a bench block or other metal surface, and tap them with a hammer to flatten. Keep tapping and testing, until you get a snug fit.

Variations

Turning a Frame into a Pendant.

It's easy to turn a delicate frame like this one into a pendant. The quickest way is to add holes for jump rings (see above, right). Before the PMC has dried, use a small straw or metal tubing to poke two holes into the top edge of the frame. If the clay is leather-hard, use a hand drill with a 1/16" (1.5 mm) bit or a Dremel tool. For both methods, reinforce the holes with doughnuts of fresh clay attached with slip.

To make the doughnuts, first roll out PMC, through plastic wrap, to a height of two cards. Use the same small straw or metal tubing you used on the frame to cut out circles of PMC. Then, use a smaller straw or tube to cut and remove the centers of the circles. Paint some slip around the holes on the frame, and position the doughnuts over the holes. Press into place, and clean up any excess slip with a clean brush. In this pendant, the holes were reinforced with

doughnuts on the front and back. If they don't complement your design, put them only on the back.

To make an alternative frame support (see above, left): When the frame is completely finished do the following: Roll a plump log of conditioned black clay approximately ½" (2.5 cm) in diameter. Trim a sectin that is about as wide as your frame. Powder the bottom edge of the frame and gently push it down in to the log of clay, stopping to repowder if it sticks. Stop about two-thirds of the way through the snake. It should stand up fairly well on its own. Make a **U**-shaped loop of wire and poke the ends in to the log to give it greater stability. Remove the frame and bake the stand according to manufacturer's directions. When it's cool you can remove the **U**-loop and adjust the fit by tapping it with a hammer as per above directions.

Bird Box Pendant

Artist: Celie Fago

Combustible support forms were used in the bead project on page 98; in this project, you will learn how to make a noncombustible support form, which is used to keep PMC from slumping during firing. The parts for this box pendant are textured and cut out of fresh clay, dried to leather-hard, then assembled with slip. Since force drying results in warpage, air dry the box parts to facilitate assembly.

Materials

- basic Precious Metal Clay equipment and supplies (see page 80)
- basic polymer clay equipment and supplies (see page 10)
- 1 ounce of standard PMC
- texture sheets
- graph paper
- foam rubber scraps
- cereal box
- small piece of paper clay or fire brick
- copy paper
- flat piece of polymer clay with transferred image, unbaked
- five-minute epoxy
- metal or plastic right angle or triangle
- round needle file
- photocopier
- jeweler's saw
- tweezers
- scrap polymer clay

Getting Started

Use a piece of plastic wrap laid over graph paper to help measure rolled-out PMC more accurately when cutting it.

1 Roll out and cut the box pieces.

Roll out about ⅛ ounce of standard PMC, through plastic wrap, to a height of four cards. Texture the clay then transfer it to a Teflon palette. Cut out a rectangle measuring 1 ¼" x 1 ⅛" (32 mm x 28.5 mm), and set it aside to dry. Repeat to make an identical rectangle, and using a craft knife, cut an opening in the rectangle. Make sure there's a ¼" (6.5 mm) border of clay on all four sides. Set aside to dry. These pieces will be the front and back of the box pendant. (See page 125 for a template diagram.)

Next, roll out ¼ ounce of clay, through plastic wrap, to a height of four cards, nudging it into a long rectangle as you roll. Texture it, then cut four ¼" (6.5 mm) wide strips that are just a little longer than the sides of the rectangles. The strips will be used for the top, the bottom, and both sides of the box; because they're slightly longer than needed, you can sand them to create a perfect fit when they're leather-hard. Set the strips aside to dry.

To make the border for the frame opening, roll out about ¼ ounce of PMC, through plastic wrap, to a height of four cards. Texture it as desired, then transfer it to a Teflon palette. Cut a rectangle from the piece that's about ⅛" (3 mm) wider all around than the frame opening. Then, cut out the center of the rectangle, leaving an ⅛" (3 mm) border.

TIP

I used a rubber stamp to texture the frame and sanding screen to texture the border for the frame opening. The sanding screen must be very well oiled, or it will trap the PMC.

NOTE

The featured piece was made using a texture with a deep relief and therefore rolled out at a #4 setting. If you use a low relief, adjust accordingly.

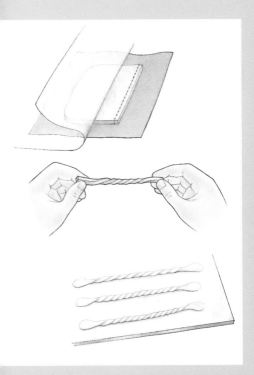

2 Make the decorative details for the box pendant.

To make twisted wires, roll out ¼ ounce of PMC, under plastic wrap, to a height of four cards. It should form a rectangle at least 2 ¼" (5 cm) long. Transfer the PMC to a Teflon palette. Using a well-oiled tissue blade, cut a strip as wide as the PMC sheet is thick so it's square. Then, gently twist the strip into a square wire. To prevent it from untwisting, firmly push both ends onto a glass surface, or other surface to which the PMC will stick, like marble or stone; be sure to remove all traces of oil. Continue making twisted wires until you have one for each side, plus a few extra in case some break. Don't worry about sizing them exactly to your box sides. Just make them a bit longer than the sides, and plan on trimming them with a protected tissue blade, once they are leather-hard. When they dry, they will detach from the glass surface on their own. Sometimes the pieces will develop a curve, but standard PMC is flexible and can be gently straightened. You may want to put the pieces under a book or other weight so they remain straight until it comes time to use them. They can also be stored, straightened, in cocktail straws. With the box seen here, the leather-hard wires were placed on the sides, bottom, and top of the box.

To make tiny spheres: Cut an extra strip from the rolled out PMC, divide it into squares, and roll four tiny spheres to decorate the corners of the box. Set them on a scrap of foam rubber to dry.

To make a bail: Pinch off a piece of PMC the size of an almond, and cut a cube measuring ¼" (6.5 mm) square. Put a hole in it using a large, well-oiled knitting needle, and set it aside to dry. As an alternative you may form the cube, let it dry, then drill a hole in it. Remember that it will shrink, so use a large needle, or at least a ¹⁄₁₆" (1.5 mm) drill bit.

3 Refine and true-up the pieces of the box pendant.

Hold the front and back pieces together, face to face, and rub the edges on 320-grit sandpaper that has been laid onto a perfectly flat surface, such as glass. Sand until the two pieces are exactly the same size. Check the corners against a right angle, and continue sanding until they're trued up and smooth. Sand the ¼" (5 mm) wide side pieces until they're true and sized to fit the rectangles. If you need to trim them first, use a protected tissue blade, which will cut through standard PMC without breaking it.

To sand the pendant opening and the border for the opening, make a small sanding tool by cutting a strip of cereal box (or equivalent) and folding 320-grit sand paper around it. This tool should be a bit narrower than the smallest dimension you're sanding. Trim and true up the twisted "wire" lengths so they're each slightly longer than the side and the bottom pieces of the box. Reserve the twisted length that will go on the top until later. Refine the cube bail by sanding it and enlarging the hole with a round needle file as necessary

4 Make a noncombustible support form.

The form, which will prevent the box from slumping as it heats up in the kiln, should be made from a nontoxic, noncombustible material. Good choices are paper clay, which is available from craft supply stores, and fire brick, a common and inexpensive material available from ceramic suppliers. Paper clay is superior to regular papier-mâché because it shrinks very little, and it can be sanded once dry, like fire brick. Because it contains volcanic ash, it won't burn up in the kiln.

The only part of the box vulnerable to slumping is the front, where the frame window is cut out. To support this area, make a form from paper clay or firebrick that is slightly larger than the window opening and 4 mm high. The easiest way to measure for your piece is to lay the box front (before assembly) on to graph paper and poke a hole at each corner. Draw a line to connect the four pin holes and make your combustible core 1 to 2 mm larger than that, all the way around, and 4 mm high.

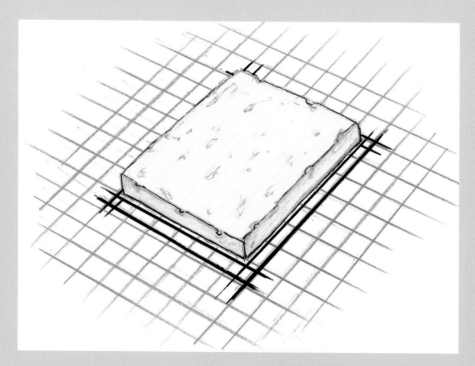

If using paper clay, sculpt it into a rectangular shape slightly larger than the size you want, and let it dry. If using fire brick, cut it slightly larger than the size you want, using a craft knife or a jeweler's saw. Then, sand the form to the size you want using 320-grit and then 400-grit sandpaper.

5 Assemble the box pendant.

Check the fit of the pieces and sand as necessary. Then, paint a line of thick, smooth slip on the back piece, along one side and along the top. Paint slip on the ends of one side piece and the top piece, then position them on the back piece, with tweezers or your fingers. If your slip is the correct consistency, these two pieces will stand up without support. Hold the pieces steady while you remove excess slip from the outside edges with a clean brush. Allow the assembly to dry completely. Attach the other ¼" (6.5 mm) side piece and let dry. Reinforce the seams as necessary from the inside, and let dry. Attach the border for the frame opening to the front piece, and let it dry. Then, attach the front piece to the three-sided assembly, and let it dry.

The bottom ¼" (6.5 mm) piece, which will be fired separately, needs to be sized now. Try the fit, and sand as necessary so that it is a little larger than the space for it. You can easily file it down after its fired, but it is a lot harder to add material if the box bottom is too small.

TIP

The bail hole can be oriented parallel to the pendant, as seen here, or perpendicular to the pendant.

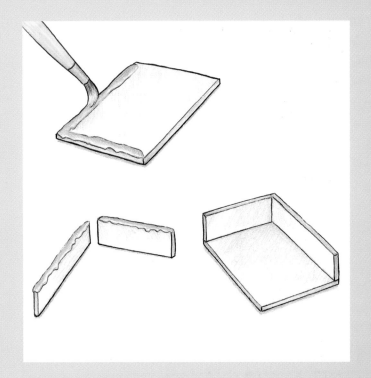

6 Attach the decorative elements and fire.

Make a pencil mark at the center of the top of the box. Attach the bail to this spot with enough thick slip so it squeezes out into a flange around the bottom of the bail. Let it dry.

Next, miter the ends of the twisted wire pieces so they meet neatly at each corner, trimming the top section as necessary to account for the bail. To miter an end, hold one twisted wire length close to the end, at an angle, and rub it gently back and forth against 320-grit sandpaper. Attach the three twisted wire sections to the box using slip, and let dry. Attach the last wire to the bottom ¼" (6.5 mm) piece using slip, and let dry. Reinforce as necessary. Attach a ball to each corner with slip.

Center the support form inside the box and place it, along with the ¼" (6.5 mm) bottom piece, in a bed of alumina hydrate or vermiculite, and fire. (See *Firing* on page 83.) Once cool, remove the support form, and finish as desired.

7 Insert the polymer clay image, and bake.

(See page 17 for more information on image transfers to polymer clay.) Slide the image into place, adding rolled-out strips of polymer clay behind the insert to fill up the area and so there's more surface area for gluing the ¼" (6.5 mm) bottom piece on after baking. Bake the whole assembly according to manufacturer's directions. Remove the polymer to sand and buff if desired, then glue it in, and the bottom piece on, using five-minute epoxy.

Gallery

Celie Fago

Exploring a new material, in this case Precious Metal Clay, can produce strikingly original work. The malleability of the clay contrasts with crisp carved textures and complex forms in these distinctive bracelets and pendants. The polymer clay elements were produced with related and visually harmonious techniques, including photo transfers and carving.

Photos: Robert Diamante

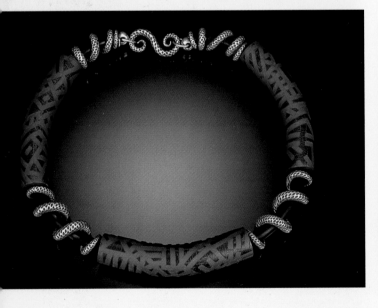

Jacqueline Lee

Love for ancient and exotic art pervades these pins and pendants. Using acrylic paint, metallic powders, and handmade molds, Lee has developed meticulous techniques to produce work that evokes the ancient Far East lacquer and wood pieces in modern clay. Elements are molded in clay, assembled and adhered with glue or TLS. *Photos: Jacqueline Lee*

Nan Roche

Mokumé gané is a versatile technique. The effects vary depending on the color, transparency, and pearlescence of the clays used. For the pieces below, a sheet made of contrasting layers of opaque clay was pressed into shallow molds and later carved or sanded away, revealing dramatic graphic patterns. A weathered look was achieved by applying a metal patina as the last step of construction. *Photos: Chris Roche*

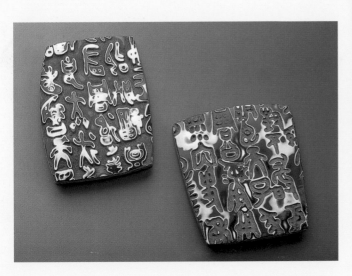

Dayle Doroshow

When is a book not a book? When it's a dream. Doroshow's evocative figurines, boxes, and plaques hold secret messages, treasures, and wishes in hidden compartments. Techniques combine sculpture, caning, doll making, and book arts. *Photos: Don Felton*

Elise Winters

This master of form and color explores new ways to combine polymer clay with other materials. The screen holds a thin sheet of tinted translucent clay embellished with gold leaf. In the cinched pin, a ring of vermeil encircles a core of subtly color-blended polymer clay and a skin crazed iridescent acrylic paint.

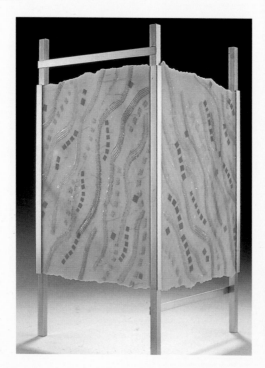

Barbara Morrison

Energy and sprit are embodied here. Wirework and beading embellish these colorful figures. *Photos: Patrick Clark*

Liz Mitchell

Polymer clay, transfer images, and paint were used to produce these distinctive books and frames. *Photos: Ralph Gabriner*

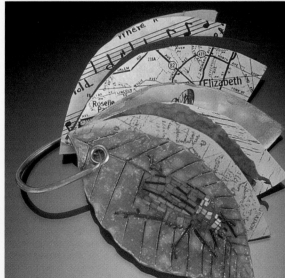

Dorothy Greynolds

These streamlined pieces make the most of the luster of pearl clays. In the pendants and earrings, paper-thin cut-out shapes in contrasting colors are applied to pearl or black bases and rolled in. *Photos: Dorothy Greynolds*

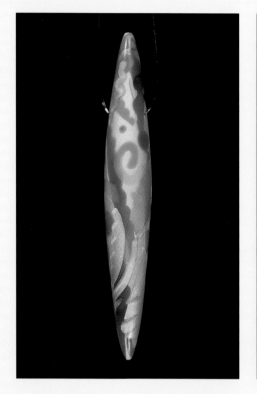

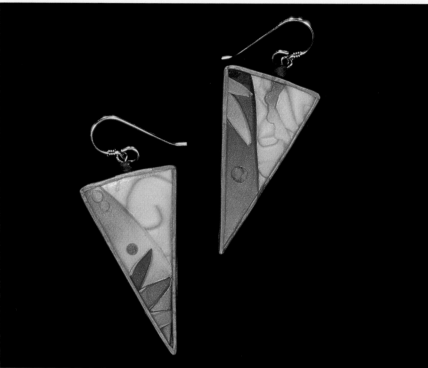

Dotty McMillan

How many decorative techniques can you spot in these Oriental looking pieces? Just for starters, the kaleidoscope employs image transfers, molded pieces, and antiquing, while the lively figures (concealing recycled prescription vials) are clothed in mokumé gané and chrysanthemum cane slices.

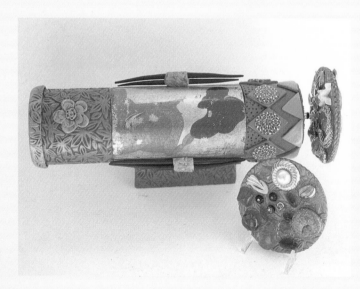

Patricia Klamser

Large, beautifully crafted evening purses bring the small traditional Japanese inro boxes into the world of modern fashion. They are formed over wooden shapes and ornamented with hand-painted and silk-screened imagery, as well as veneers featuring metallic clay effects, carving, and texturing. *Photos: Rob Vinnedge*

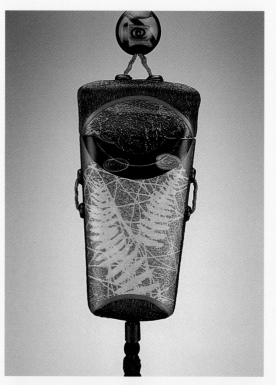

Judy Kuskin

In these unusual mixed-media necklaces and wall pieces, found objects like driftwood, shells, and feathers contrast with polymer clay design elements. These diverse pieces employ many techniques, including carving, backfilling with contrasting-colored clay, molding, texturing, mokumé gané, canework, crackling, patinas, and antiquing. *Photos: Roger Schrieber*

Liz Tamayo

Voyages of imagination, discovery, and delight are memorialized in these complex hinged albums. The "postcards" are polymer clay, too, and made with transfers as well as paint and patinas. *Photos: Don Felder*

Gwen Gibson

Innovation is Gibson's hallmark, from the Tear-Away technique "cave art" brooch to the silk-screened lentil beads, bracelet, and pendant. The transfer image on the pendant (lower left) was made on the back of a paper-thin sheet of translucent clay, tinted, laid over crackled metal leaf on clay, baked, and highly polished. *Photos: Robert Diamonte*

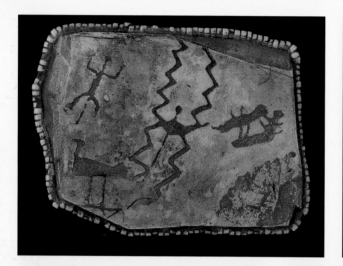

Maj-Britt Cawthon

Polymer clay adapts just as easily to bold, geometric modern designs as it does to traditional imagery and imitating ancient artifacts. Mokumé gané and simple canes are used to decorate the big, bold, elegant beads in these necklaces. *Photos: John Bonath*

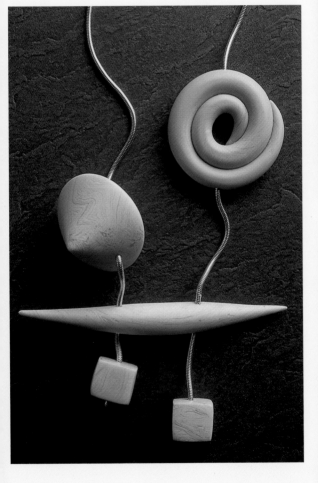

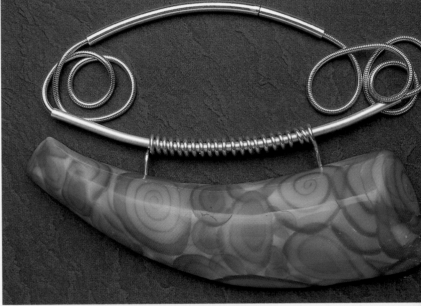

Standard PMC Frame Project Templates

Textured Silver Frame with Inset
(see page 106)

These templates show the before and after firing sizes of five sample rectangles. The larger size in each set (left) represents the "before firing" size. The smaller size in each set (right) shows the 28% shrinkage of standard PMC. If you roll standard PMC out to a height of 3 cards, you'll use approximately the portion of an ounce listed under each "before firing" size.

¾ of an oz.

¼ of an oz.

between ¼ and ⅓ oz.

⅛ of an oz.

½ of an oz.

Diagram for Cutting Accurate Frame Windows

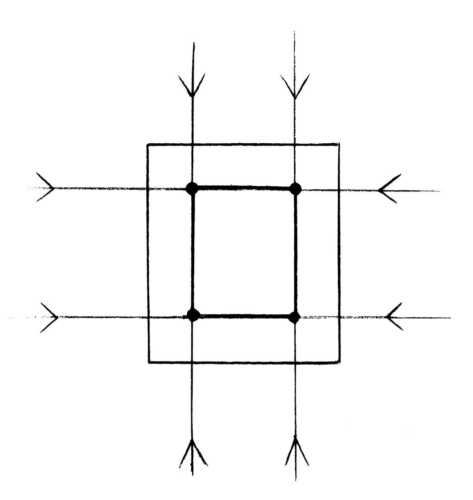

Bird Box Pendant (see page 110)

Use a diagram like the one shown here to help cut
the window accurately. Cut the rectangle for the
front of the box and place it on a scrap of plastic.
Position it precisely on the diagram and follow the
arrow lines in at each corner to find the spot to
poke the four holes. Then, using a craft knife, cut
the window out using the four holes as guides.

Contributing Artists

Authors

Celie Fago
RR 1 Box 376
Bethel, VT 05032
806-234-5428
E-mail: celie@adelphia.net

Livia McRee
E-mail: livia@liviamcree.com

Georgia Sargeant
2400 Virginia Ave. NW, #C-1017
Washington, DC 20037
202-223-0777
E-mail: georgiapeach@erols.com

Project Artists

Meredith Arnold
Moonenstars Unlimited
110 N. 201 St.
Shoreline, WA 98133-3012
206-542-3405
E-mail: marnold@nwlink.com

Jody Bishel
548 Wakelee Ave.
Ansonia, CT 06401-1226
203-735-5879
E-mail: jbishel@aol.com

Dan Cormier
RR1, Site 24, C67
Gabriola Island, BC V0R 1X0
CANADA
E-mail: hoco@island.net

Dayle Doroshow
Zingaro
P.O. Box 354
Fort Bragg, CA 95437
707-962-9419
E-mail:
dayledoroshow@hotmail.com

Linda Goff
1204 S. Fir
Olympia, WA 98501
E-mail: Wire4Clay2@aol.com

Susan Hyde
Susan Hyde Designs
3920 Sunnyside Ave. N.
Seattle, WA 98103
206-281-1559
E-mail: shd2clay@aol.com

Jacqueline Lee
1645 S. 350 E.
Springville, UT 84663
801-489-6226
E-mail: jacquelinelee@mail.com

Ellen Marshall
2420 Montrose St.
Philadelphia, PA 19146
215-752-0360
E-mail: larrine@msn.com

Elissa Powell
Elissahearts
1731 Santa Cruz Ave.
Santa Clara, CA 95051
E-mail: elissahearts@yahoo.com

Margaret F. H. Reid
2 Stone House
Howey
Llandrindod Wells
Powys LD1 5PL
UNITED KINGDOM
(44) 1597 825517
E-mail:
mfhreid@polyopol.kc3ltd.co.uk

Leigh S. Ross
Polymer Clay Central
610 5th Ave.
Bradley Beach, NJ 07720
732-776-6576
E-mail: sincereleigh@polymerclay-central.com

Gallery Artists

Maj-Britt Cawthon
11715 West 18th Ave.
Lakewood, CO 80215
303-274-7565
E-mail: mbcawthon@att.net

Dayle Doroshow
P.O. Box 354
Ft. Bragg, CA 95437
707-962-9419
E-mail:
dayledoroshow@hotmail.com

Gwen Gibson
216 Bayview St.
San Rafael, CA 94901
415-454-3241
E-mail: gwen@gwengibson.com

Dorothy Greynolds
5678 Eldridge Dr.
Waterford, MI 48327
248-683-1107
E-mail: claywear@yahoo.com

Patricia Klamser
308 20th Ave. S.
Seattle, WA 98144
206-322-8819
E-mail: pklamser@hotmail.com

Judy Kuskin
2527 32nd Ave. S.
Seattle, WA 9814
206-725-2725
E-mail: jkuskin@hotmail.com

Jacqueline Lee
1645 South 350 East
Springville, UT 84663
801-489-6033
E-mail: jacquelinelee@mail.com

Dotty McMillan
7060 Fireside Dr.
Riverside, CA 92506
909-780-4056
dmcmillan01@earthlink.net

Liz Mitchell
101 Upper Kingtown Rd.
Pittstown, NJ 08867
908-735-5710
E-mail: lizzez@ptd.net

Barbara Morrison
717 Hiberta St.
Missoula, MT 59804
406-721-6159
E-mail: tmw717@hotmail.com

Nan Roche
4511 Amherst Rd.
College Park, MD 20740
301-864-1805
E-mail: nan@nanroche.com

Liz Tamayo
2926 Holyrood Dr.
Oakland, CA 94611
510-530-7249
E-mail: LizzeeT@aol.com

Elise Winters
56 Adams Ave.
Haworth, NJ 07641
201- 501-0520
E-mail: winterse@aol.com

Resources

Polymer Clay, Tools, and Supplies

United States

Accent Import Export, Inc.
1501 Loveridge Rd. Box 16
Pittsburg, CA 94565
Phone: 1-800-989-2889
E-mail: sean@fimozone.com
Web site: www.fimozone.com
General supplies, "Magic Leaf" patterned
leaf, molds, stamps, books, crackle finishes,
and adhesives

American Art Clay Co. Inc.
4717 W. 16th St.
Indianapolis, IN 46222
Phone: 1-800-374-1600
Fax: 317-248-9300
E-mail: amacobrent@aol.com;
catalog@amaco.com
Web site: www.amaco.com
General supplies, push molds, tools

Clay Factory, Inc.
P.O. Box 460598
Escondido, CA 92046-0598
Phone: 877-728-5739
E-mail: clayfactoryinc@clayfactoryinc.com
Web site: www.clayfactoryinc.com
General supplies, Cernit, ripple blades

Mindstorm Productions, Inc.
2625 Alcatraz Ave., Suite 241
Berkeley, CA 94705
Phone: 510-644-1952
Fax: 510-644-3910
E-mail: burt@mindstorm-inc.com
Web site: www.mindstorm-inc.com
Instructional videos

Polymer Clay Express
13017 Wisteria Dr., Box 275
Germantown, MD 20874
Phone: 1-800-844-0138
Fax: 301-482-0610
Web site: www.polymerclayexpress.com
General supplies, hard-to-find items

Prairie Craft Company
P.O. Box 209
Florissant, CO 80816-0209
Phone: 1-800-779-0615
Fax: 719-748-5112
E-mail: vernon@pcisys.net
Web site: www.prairiecraft.com
General supplies, Liquid Sculpey,
"NuBlade Kato" and "Marxit Kato" tools

Red Castle, Inc.
Phil Schloss
P.O. Box 39-8001
Edina, MN 55439-8001
Phone: 877-733-2278
Web site: www.red-castle.com
"Fit-It" templates of specialty boxes
and other forms, on CD-ROM

United Kingdom

American Art Clay Co. Inc.
P.O. Box 467
Longton
Stoke-On-Trent, ST3 7DN
Phone: (44) 01782 399219
Fax: (44) 01782 394891
E-mail: andrewcarter@amaco.uk.co
Web site: www.amaco.uk.co
General supplies, push molds, tools

Homecrafts Direct
P.O. Box 247
Leicester, LE1 9QS
Phone: (44) 0116 251 0405
E-mail: post@speccrafts.co.uk
Web site: www.speccrafts.co.uk
General supplies, Formello, tools, cold enamels

The Polymer Clay Pit
British Polymer Clay Guild
Meadow Rise, Low Rd.
Wortham, Diss
Norfolk, IP22 1SQ
Phone: (44) 01379 646019
Fax: (44) 0139 646016
E-mail: claypit@heaser.demon.co.uk
Web site: www.heaser.demon.co.uk/claypit.htm
General supplies, Creall-therm

Precious Metal Clay

Metalliferous Inc.
34 West 46th St.
New York, NY 10036
Phone: 1-888-944-0909
Jewelry tools and supplies, unusual findings

PMC Tool and Supply
1 Feeder St.
Lambertville, NJ 08530
Phone: 609-397-9550
PMC supplies, kiln supplies, videos

Rio Grande
7500 Bluewater Rd. N.W.
Albuquerque, NM 87121
Phone: 1-800-545-6566
PMC, PMC supplies, kilns and kiln supplies,
craft videos, jewelry tools, findings

Organizations

United States

National Polymer Clay Guild
PMB 345
1350 Beverly Rd., 115
McLean, VA 22101
Web site: www.npcg.org

PMC Guild
417 W. Mountain Ave.
Fort Collins, CO 80521
Phone: 970-419-5503
E-mail: office@PMCguild.com
Web site: www.PMCguild.com
Information about PMC and
PMC Certification Classes

United Kingdom

British Polymer Clay Guild
Meadow Rise, Low Rd.
Wortham, Diss
Norfolk, IP22 1SQ
E-mail: bpcg@heaser.demon.co.uk
Web site: www.heaser.demon.co.uk/
  poly-clay/guild/britpol.htm

About the Authors

Georgia Sargeant started drawing, sewing, and building things as a child and never stopped. After studying studio arts in college, she became a graphic artist, reporter, and editor. From 1997 to 2001 she was the editor of the quarterly newsletter of the National Polymer Clay Guild, where she featured and wrote about leading polymer clay artists from around the world. She has been working with polymer clay for over a decade and loves to learn and teach new techniques.

Celie Fago began working in polymer clay in 1991 after years of working as a painter and sculptor. Her jewelry combines polymer with metalworking and with Precious Metal Clay. She's a highly regarded, generous, and innovative teacher who has done groundbreaking work combining these materials. She's one of six senior instructors of Precious Metal Clay worldwide and was invited by master metalsmith Tim McCreight to be Mitsubishi's PMC Liaison to the polymer clay community in 1999. Celie and Tim's intermediate video, *Push Play for PMC* is available from the author or where craft videos are sold.

Livia McRee is a craft designer and writer, and a former editor at *Handcraft Illustrated* magazine. She's author of *Easy Transfers for Any Surface: Crafting with Images and Photos; Quick Crafts: 30 Fast and Fun Projects;* and *Instant Fabric: Quilted Projects from Your Home Computer.* Her work has been published online, and she has contributed to several how-to craft books.

Acknowledgments

Georgia Sargeant

Putting together this book was like throwing a big party with a lot of help from friends. The polymer clay community, as always, came through in style, and I am grateful to everyone who contributed. Many thanks to the artists who generously gave their time, expertise, imagination, and passion to produce projects that show us how to make delightful household items and jewelry while we learn important techniques. Many thanks to the artists who sent in slides of work for the gallery section—work that both delights us and opens up further ways to use the techniques from the projects. I won't list them all here; you will meet them in the gallery section. Many thanks to Celie Fago for her artistry, her pioneering work in Precious Metal Clay, and her willingness to invite us all to explore how to use it with polymer clay. Many thanks to Livia McRee, who gallantly put together all the bits and made sure everything was in place. Many thanks to Mary Ann Hall, who asked me to host this party, and to Regina Grenier, the art director who created the overall look of the book. Many thanks to Elise Winters for letting me pore over her slide collection in search of artwork that would show wonderful applications for these techniques. My special personal thanks to two wonderful artists and teachers, Tory Hughes and Nan Roche, who started me on my journey of discovery in the wonderful world of polymer clay, kindling my imagination and empowering my heart and hands.

Celie Fago

I would like to thank the following for their contribution of materials to this book effort: The Mitsubishi Material Corp., Sanda, Japan; CeCe Wire and the PMC Guild, Fort Collins CO; and Rio Grande, Albuquerque, NM. Personally I'd like to thank my apprentice Jennifer Kahn for all her help; my parents, D'ann Calhoun Fago and Vincent Fago for their encouragement; and Tim McCreight for his support.

Livia McRee

Many thanks to the wonderful staff at Rockport Publishers. Your style, enthusiasm, and grace under pressure doesn't go unnoticed.